# *Author*

Pete Langford was born in Durham, on April 10th, 1943. After a few months he was brought to Leighton Buzzard, where he has spent the rest of his life.

His mother Cissie, a miner's daughter, came from Sacriston, County Durham and his late father was a Tottenham boy who, during the war, served in the oldest regiment in Britain 'The Honourable Artillery Company'.

Grandad Langford was a Detective Inspector at Old Scotland Yard and retired to a pub in Leighton Buzzard. It was at that pub that Pete spent his infancy, holding his nose from the smell of beer.

The family moved, but only a few hundred yards away, opposite Leopold Road Secondary Modern School, where, much to his regret in later years, he somewhat neglected his education.

When he was fifteen years old he began writing songs and he is now working on his second book.

His twenty-eight-year-old daughter Tanya has recently presented him with a grand-daughter, Eve, a time-consuming pleasure.

While writing this story, shouts of "Dinner's Ready!"
went in one ear and out the other. Giving myself
deadlines ruined many a beautiful meal.
I dedicate this book to my wife Veronica
with love, Joe

# ONCE A KNIGHT

## THE HISTORY OF THE BARRON KNIGHTS

WRITTEN BY

## PETE LANGFORD

International Music Publications Ltd
Bookshop Sales Division
Southend Road
Woodford Green
Essex IG8 8HN
England

Published in Great Britain in 1993

ISBN 1–85909–082–6

Typeset by Datix International Ltd, Bungay, Suffolk NR35 1EF
in 12/15pt Monophoto Bembo
Reprographics by PDQ Repro Ltd, Bungay, Suffolk
Printed in England by Clays Ltd, St Ives plc

# *Foreword*

The Sixties was an extremely fertile period for pop music with new groups springing up like weeds in a window box. Usually they would burst onto the scene with a hit record and a string of TV appearances. But with few exceptions, after one or two hits they were unable to sustain their success and faded away to become, in later years, subjects perhaps of 'Where are they now?' articles.

One group stood out from all the others back then, not only because they were incredibly handsome and extremely talented, sorry, I meant NOT because they were incredibly handsome and talented, but because they skilfully combined pop music and comedy, putting new and amusing lyrics to pop hits of the day. The combination proved a potent one giving them a string of hit records and many loyal fans. Their live performances have always been so good and have simply got better and better.

Creativity, hard work, professionalism and talent have all played their part in achieving and sustaining the success still enjoyed by the Barron Knights.

Good on you lads.

Hank Marvin. A fan.

It's about time something was written about the Barron Knights.

For years, they have kept alive the spirit of entertainment and at all venues they have fostered goodwill and bonhomie with a polished performance second to none. It has been my pleasure to work with the boys on several occasions and it's been an absolute delight to watch and hear them 'Wow' an audience.

May they continue to keep afloat the essence of variety.

Les Dawson

Les sent this to me on the 9th June, 1993. He sadly passed away the following day.

I am delighted to have been invited to pen the foreword to this rib-tickling tome. The Barron Knights have just celebrated 30 years in show business, which means they're either very lucky or very talented. They've played every theatre and club in the country and helped to keep variety alive and well.

I first met this quick-witted quintet in 1965, a particularly good year for Merseyside. Liverpool won the FA Cup for the first time, the Beatles met the Maharishi and Yours Truly became the proud possessor of a golden disc for my Number One hit recording, *Tears*.

I was due to open at the London Palladium and when I saw the lads busking to the queue outside my local labour exchange, I realised their magical gift and what a great asset they would be to the show. With the Barron Knights on the bill we would have more people on the stage than in the audience! And how's this for a coincidence? The name of the singer, Duke D'mond is actually an anagram of Ken Dodd, MU (Musicians Union); but we're not related in any way.

What started as a 4-week season stretched into a fantastically successful 42 weeks and their side-splitting send-ups of the top pop groups played a huge part in our record-breaking run. Their impressions were hilarious, their parodies witty, they were musically gifted – and they had the customers in stitches. Yes, even then I was beginning to dislike them.

It was hard work. Twice nightly, three times on a Saturday – and we had to turn up at the theatre too! But we were young, virile and fit in those days. If my memory serves me correctly we had 25 dancing girls in the show. What it was to see five strapping young lads degenerate into a shuffling group of bent, trembling sexagenarians.

The Barron Knights first blossomed in the Sixties, the era of Flower Power. Many of the groups that emerged then have gone to seed, but the boys are still as bright and as fresh as a daisy. I think it's sleeping with their feet in a bucket of compost that does it! In the Hallowed Halls of British Buffoonery some say they've become an institution, many others say they belong in one.

Pete Langford, who was there at the Palladium in the Swinging Sixties, writes lots of fabulous songs for the Knights. They've had hit records like *Call Up The Groups* . . . unforgettable classics including *Don't Let The Germans Pinch Your Sunbed*, *Pop Go The Workers* and *Merry Gentle Pops*. They've become legends in their own Happy Hour.

And here they are today, thirty years on and still bonded together. The years have been kind to them. Onwards through the Nineties they're still charging forward like bold knights of old, lances poised to puncture pomposity with their peerless parodies and take-offs.

True, when they're not on stage they go their own separate ways. Duke has the castor oil concession for the Olympics, Pete (who used to look like 'Bubbles' in the Pears soap ads) now models for slag heaps, and Butch Baker, another founder member, is a stunt man in a Punch and Judy show. Meanwhile, Barron happily pours over his collection of bent pieces of wire, but Dave, I'm sorry to say, has fallen into evil ways. He's become a theatrical agent.

It can't have been easy compiling this book, when four of the five lads still sign autograph books with a cross. They were hoping to employ a ghost writer, but they couldn't get Bram Stoker to come through on the Ouija board! Luckily, one of them still has his Janet and John books, so he penned this narrative while the others stood around admiring his joined-up writing.

But as I say, I'm delighted – and honoured – to have been asked to make this small contribution to the Barron Knights' story. They're smashing lads, and if their act is anything to go by, this book is going to tittilate your chuckle muscles for a long time to come.

Ken Dodd

# *Preface*

In 1984, we were in Guernsey to perform at a private function for the sales force of 'Snap On Tools'. We had been booked for the show a whole year in advance and we were to be kept a secret until the moment the lights hit the stage!

We arrived in the afternoon and were taken to a near-by hotel to rehearse our purpose-written songs. An hour before the show, we were driven to the function, where we were given a tiny little dressing room at the opposite end of the room to the stage . . . The normal pre-show tension was building slowly.

The audience were as eager to see their little surprise as we were excited to present them with one!

There was to be a blackout and that would be our cue to find a pathway through the tables, hop onto the stage and hit the first chord. Dead on time, the lights went down and we started our journey, threading our way to the stage. When we were no more than two paces away, we heard this female voice with a southern accent say, 'Ere Alf, who do you think it is?' and Alf replied, 'It looks like the Barron Knights'. 'Jesus Christ,' she said, 'are they still alive?'

I finished this book in March, 1993. In the January and February we were filling theatres around the UK, so I'm pleased to say that we are very much alive and kicking . . . very hard! If you're not appearing on television these days, the majority of people think that you are dead; but there are people who enjoy a live show and we have spent over thirty years working hard to make ours a hard act to follow.

When I decided that I wanted to be in a pop group, I was worried about the insecurity of such a career; so was Dad.

However, I took the opportunities that were offered and they gave me much more than just a little financial security.

This book contains no sex, drugs or even murder, but there's many a funny story and it is the history of a band that has been, and still is, my life.

As I was writing each page, I realised that I had experienced most emotions: excitement, depression, happiness, sadness, failure and success, but most of all the burning desire to keep the band working to a high standard. I will want to do something else if we let that standard drop and that will be the end of a bunch of guys that gave the world a bag full of innocent laughs.

We toured with the Beatles, the Stones were our support band and we even influenced Bill Wyman to become a bass player. Although we were a comedy band, we were very much a part of the Sixties scene and then went on to make the Seventies our biggest record-selling period.

My thanks go to the hotel rooms from Warrington to Auckland, for giving me a page a day.

# Mr Gibbins

In 1958 I didn't really know what I wanted to do in life; who does, when they're fifteen years old? Every morning at 4.30 am, I used to bike to Southcott Stud and muck out, feed and water twelve hunter horses. They belonged to Bill Lewis the stable owner, whose face was like a walnut and whose liver must have begged for a good drop of highland spring water. Watering the horses was the worst job, because carrying two full pails on a freezing cold morning with half of the water slopping down your wellies was no joke. Perhaps that's why I never saw a smile on the faces of his two daughters, Joan and Mary. I subsequently abandoned the ambition of becoming a famous show-jumper. The stables have now been replaced by a cul-de-sac of bungalows, but each time I drive past, I still smell the tack room and dung heap and probably will for the rest of my life.

At 7.30 am I did a paper round for Mr Stubberfield and I passed all the sour-faced men going to work at the Foundry Equipment or catching the bus to Vauxhall Motors in Dunstable – could that be me in a few years' time?

In addition to the paper round, I delivered fruit and vegetables for Mr Cornish and meat for Mr Yirrell. One of my favourite jobs, however, was a Saturday morning errand for Mr Gibbins, who lived a few doors along the road. The poor man suffered so badly with asthma, that when he breathed, you looked up to make sure a Spitfire wasn't flying low overhead. It was a bad case. To assist his breathing, he needed a weekly supply of the drug Fennox, and that was my job to fetch the medicine from Boots. I remember that it cost 2/6 and Mr Gibbins always gave me sixpence for a job well done.

Mr Gibbins had something that few homes had in those days . . . a television. When I handed him his little package, he always had the front door wide open and I could spot the magic box. Sometimes it was switched on, which was even more fascinating. I always was a determined little brat and if I wanted something, I never gave up until I got it. At that time, to watch TV was my one ambition. I didn't care what was on, just to sit there and be mesmerised by what was on the screen would be wonderful.

Every Sunday morning most fathers went to the pub for a well-earned pint or two, (or in my Dad's case three or four, plus a wee nip). About 2 pm Mum would ask me to go to the top of the hill to see if Dad was on his way home. Once I had spotted him, I would rush back and that was her cue for putting the Yorkshire puddings in the oven. From a quarter of a mile away Dad was easy to spot. He had both hands in his pockets, smoke billowing from his mouth like the Royal Scot and his walk was that of a thinking man. My viewing point was from right outside Mr Gibbins's gate, where, if it wasn't raining, he would stand and pass the time of day with his neighbours. This was when I seized the opportunity to ask if I could come in to watch the telly.

'What do you want to watch? I go to bed early.' As I looked up into the sky and realised there were no Spitfires, I replied, 'Sunday Night at the London Palladium.'

I could hardly eat my dinner, I was so excited. When I told Mum, she informed me that Slim Whitman was appearing with Tommy Trinder – she would have loved to have seen it.

By 7.30 pm, I was rooted to a chair in Mr Gibbins's lounge with his son Dick and Mrs Gibbins. Because Mr Gibbins was slightly deaf, he had the volume up high, which was great because it rode above the sound of the Spitfires! Once the show had started, I couldn't believe my eyes. Across the whole of the stage there were at least twenty dancing girls with extremely long legs. (They reminded me of a row of swiss army knives, with all their gadgets open.) The atmosphere in the theatre seemed to permeate through the screen into Mr Gibbins's front room. First, Tommy Trinder appeared wearing a funny hat and told a few jokes; then, after three jugglers and another singer, he announced in his cockney accent, 'From America, Slim Whitman'. My eyes popped out like organ stops. Although I noticed his cowboy look, tassles hanging from his shirt, string tie and greased-back hair, I was struck by the sight of this beautiful blonde! Sparkling in the spotlight was his guitar. That was it! From that day forward, I had no other thoughts except of playing the guitar at the Palladium.

I did learn to play, much to the regret of our next-door neighbours. With the Barron Knights, I performed on a few 'Sunday Nights at the London Palladium' and every night for 26 weeks in 1965 with the brilliant Ken Dodd. The show broke all attendance records in the history of the theatre. Unfortunately, Mr Gibbins never saw the results of his neighbourly gesture. In 1960 the Spitfire passed peacefully away!

## *Meeting Butch*

With the little money that I had, I bought a mandoline from Spud Murphy which had belonged to his late father. Although Spud was no more than five feet three, he weight-trained with a kitchen chair for two years and ended up with a body like Charles Atlas! All he was interested in was his motor bike and restoring an old sports car, so parting with the mandoline wasn't a problem for him. It cost me seven pounds. I cheated slightly by tuning it like a guitar and from the ubiquitous Bert Weedon's *Play in a Day* book, I taught myself enough chords to play and sing *Oh Rose Marie*, Slim Whitman's big hit. I also learned the famous Spanish classic *Malaguena*. Despite selling me the mandoline, Spud is still a very good friend of all the Barron Knights.

'Keep that bloody noise down.' Mr & Mrs Buchanan, our wall-tapping neighbours, were driven mad as I repeated the same tunes day in and day out. They were post office workers, rising early and coming home for an afternoon nap, which was not a good routine to have while living next door to a budding rock'n'roll star. Our other neighbour, Frances Saunders, used to sunbathe on her back lawn while I practised upstairs with my window wide open. It wasn't until I met her twenty years later in Sydney, Australia, that she revealed how little she had enjoyed the fruits of my limited talents. I always wondered why she emigrated!

I was finding it hard to improve my playing of the mandoline but one day I seized the opportunity to play a real guitar. It belonged to a youth from the village of Pitstone, seven miles from my home in Linslade, Leighton Buzzard. The first time that I set eyes on Butch Baker was when he climbed through the ground floor window of the Hunt Hotel in Linslade. I was a friend of the hotel owners' son, a bespectacled, posh kid with the equally posh name of Simon Wesley. We used to have great parties when we danced to Elvis and Marty Wilde records. One of these parties was on a boiling hot summer night, when all the windows were open wide; so in popped Butch, sang a few Lonnie Donegan songs, had a dance and climbed out again.

While he was dancing, I 'plonked' a few chords on this gigantic, blonde Hofner guitar . . . Wow! That was it!

Despite my Dad refusing to sign any HP forms, I bought a

beautiful Hoya guitar. It was even better than Butch's Hofner and you couldn't keep me away from it; we were inseparable.

My musical education was, to say the least, limited. Hearing Mum sing along to 'Workers' Playtime' or 'Family Favourites', was all that home had to offer. If Dad's singing voice had been as good as his sense of humour, he would have outshone Bing Crosby. Brother Dave was always tapping things, much to our annoyance, and my younger brother Denis and sister Margaret were too young to want to know about treble clefs and minims. At school, we had a music lesson once a week, which unfortunately hardly complied with the Trades Descriptions Act! Every Tuesday morning, after Assembly, the headmaster, Mr 'Taffy' Jenkins carried the school record player into the hall. Having wound it up, he carefully placed a 78 rpm record of *Jupiter* from Holst's *Planet Suite* onto the turntable and nervously scratched across the record with the needle, before sitting down for a well-earned rest. During my later years at Linslade Secondary Modern, we were granted the benefit of a music teacher who could play the piano. Mr Radford seemed to be aware of my interest in the subject and took us one step further and made us sing songs to his accompaniment.

Being a member of St Barnabas Church Choir was most informative as well as fun. Lionel Claydon, the choirmaster, was very strict when it came to musical time-keeping and I discovered that descant and counter melodies were very tough to learn. Although we were drilled very hard every Monday and Friday evening, I loved every minute and was rewarded for my enthusiasm when Mr Claydon gave me the Head Boy's Ribbon to wear around my neck. Once a month, at Sunday Evensong I performed my party piece *Oh, For The Wings Of A Dove*. Of course, the annual day out at Wicksteed Park, near Northampton, was another attraction to choir singing!

Thirty-five years on, I now regret that my parents didn't

*Choirboy (second from left), 1957.*

push me harder in the direction of music, or glue me onto a piano stool and make me play! Dad worked as hard as any man could, even to the extent of working on a farm during his holiday so that we could all have our extra treats. But a piano was out of the question. On many hot summer days, I would sit in the back yard and play the theme tune from *Tom Thumb* on the mouth organ, but it didn't give me the musical satisfaction I needed.

Once I had discovered that Butch worked for the local newspaper, it didn't take long for him to get totally fed up with me constantly popping into his office and asking him to show me the chords of all the latest songs. Over the next few weeks, despite my pestering, we struck up a great friendship, but, as I was to discover, he could be very unreliable. Butch was a very heavy smoker, he liked his pint and most of all, partygoing. Nothing stood in the way of the latter and it was quite common for me to bike over to Pitstone on a Sunday morning, with my guitar over the handlebars, only to find him either still in bed or just arriving home from a party in Berkhampstead.

Towards the end of 1958, Butch and I were gaining a small reputation for our playing and singing. (The standard around Leighton Buzzard obviously wasn't too high.) I'd be playing in local coffee bars as well as at Linslade Youth Club, while Butch frequented pubs and parties. His repertoire consisted mostly of dirty rugby songs and any Elvis song you could name. We would occasionally get together at the 'Clarendon' pub in Linslade and team up with Johnny Wilson, another guitarist, who was also the proud owner of the loudest voice in Buckinghamshire. It seemed that any night that *we* were there, so was the whole of the town. There wasn't an Elvis or Lonnie song we couldn't sing and by performing the Everleys' songs, I learned how to harmonize. Those nights with Butch and Johnny were so important to me, because in reality we were a three piece group.

Dad was very unsure about his second son not having a secure job in engineering. To him, what I was doing was an unknown quantity and he saw no future for me, just my enthusiasm and dedication to pop music. He insisted that I found a 'proper' job and glancing through the local paper I noticed a vacancy for a sewing machine mechanic with a company called Gossards (makers of bras and suspenders). Before I could say 'Wee Willie Harris', I was one of only two males in a factory of about sixty women and fifty sewing machines. I never did find out who made the most noise, the women or the machines, but I soon became both an expert at changing their needles and very confident in women's company. As a career at Gossards was a frightening prospect, I became even more determined to pursue my desire. I practised day and night until my fingers bled – and one day they really did – when a sewing machine fell onto my fingers and I lost the top of my right forefinger. That was enough, I was off!

## The Talent Show

Linslade Youth Club received a letter asking if any member would like to enter the 'Frankie Vaughan Youth Talent Competition'. There wasn't much of a choice of applicants (unless they accepted synchronised light ale drinkers!) but I couldn't wait to apply. I mentioned it to Butch and, as long as it didn't interfere with his partying, he was willing to take part: so we formed a duo. Our programme consisted of two instrumentals. Butch played *Guitar Boogie*, while I played the accompanying chords, then he walked off stage while I played *Malaguena* . . . with only three fingers!

The first round of the competition was in the beautiful Buckinghamshire town of Olney, where we won easily and gained a place in the area finals in Aylesbury. What happened in the next few weeks will never be erased from my memory. The Aylesbury show was on a Saturday and on the previous Thursday, I met Butch biking home with his Hofner strapped to his back with baling string. Very calmly and without any hint of apology, he told me he couldn't make the show after all, because he would be going to a party in Tring! I thought I was having a nightmare! I didn't show how hurt I was, but inside I was on the verge of tears. At the age of 16 and 'tunnel-visioned' about being a pop star, I had thought that we were on our way, then bang! How could he miss such an opportunity? Over and over again I asked myself the same question. Where was the dedication? How could a guy who played the guitar so well, choose a party in Tring in favour of stardom?

Although my plans seemed to have been totally destroyed, I had an idea in the back of my mind. I could play *Guitar Boogie*, but I needed a partner to play the rhythm chords of E, A & B7th . . . Brain storm . . . Brother Dave. He was a bit ropey but what choice did I have? I raced to the railway station and met him off the train from Wolverton where he was a pupil at College. He listened to my plea and I received my second shock of the day when he said 'Yes'. After one and a bit days, Dave knew exactly when to change chords: it was when I nodded.

As the time grew closer, he was beginning to regret his decision. I detected nerves: you could never get into the lav at home!

When we arrived at the school hall in Aylesbury, the stage was covered with drums and amplifiers. I had never witnessed such a sight. It was obvious that there were a few groups in the show and after rehearsals I realised that we hadn't a hope in hell of winning, but I could sense that groups were the future. One thing I did notice was that the guitarists were no better than me, maybe worse. 'Butch, you fool, where the hell are you? Here I am with four fingers on one hand, three on the other and a brother who keeps wanting to shit!'

Evening came, time for the show and I was worried about Dave. He was looking like a frightened ghost. A singer and a boy-wonder magician, (with whom I was impressed until his baby rabbit panicked, jumped off the table and ran off stage), were followed by one of the groups. They were a terrific hit with their ninety-seven coach loads of followers (envy was creeping in) then it was our turn.

*Guitar Boogie* went very well but Dave's legs shook visibly. He leaned on the left leg, that started up; he changed to the right leg and that one also gave every impression of being a pneumatic drill. As planned, he walked off stage and I went into *Malaguena*. Although we were given great support, it was obvious that a group was going to win the day. When I walked off the stage, I was expecting to see Dave, but he was nowhere to be seen. Being concerned, I went off to look for him and found such a sad sight. There he was, my big brother, a county footballer with a strapping, strong physique, throwing up over a concrete pillar. He's never forgiven me to this day. He never even sends me a birthday card and he certainly never wanted to be in a rock'n'roll band.

# The Barron Knights

I was employed at Gossards bra factory for a whole year and it was like a prison sentence. The people were great, but I didn't want that kind of life. So I drifted from wood-yard to record shop, making garden sheds for five and a half days a week and helping in Reynolds the local record shop on a Saturday afternoon. Frustration was setting in and I was desperate to get out of Leighton Buzzard. Butch and I would occasionally play together and then out of the blue, he dealt me another blow. He informed me that he was off to live in London and work for a magazine called 'Engineering'.

I carried on practising my guitar-playing and sent a tape to the BBC, who sent it back with a formal letter of apology. I auditioned for a dance band, and failed because I couldn't read music quickly enough. In desperation, I was considering quite seriously of emigrating to Australia. One of my friends had been there for a year and was loving it.

Life consisted of going to the Youth Club three times a week, then down to the 'White Horse' for a light ale and walking home with brother Dave. But one night the 'White Horse' pub did me a big favour. Dave had always fancied himself as a drummer. At the all-night jazz club in the Grosvenor dance hall in Aylesbury, he always stood in the front when Terry Lightfoot's drummer did a twenty-minute solo; then he would come home and start tapping things until Mum went bananas. Then one Tuesday morning after breakfast, Dave spotted an advert for a drummer in our local paper. (Mum only bought the paper to see who had died and every week there was always someone she knew who had passed on to the 'non-paying tax home'.) When it was my turn for the paper, I noticed that the ad. had been ripped out, but I didn't put too much importance on it.

The following Saturday, Dave and I and the usual gang strode the two hundred yards from the Youth Club to the 'White Horse' and had our usual light ales until the landlord called time. On the way home, Dave took out the ad from his top pocket, went to the phone box and in no time at all had arranged for someone to audition him for the drummer's job.

11

Was he mad? No – Benskins brewery had spoken in his absence!

On a bright Sunday morning in April, 1960 the Langford family greeted Anthony Michael John Osmond into their home. In his mid-twenties, with a public school-educated voice, he was extremely self-assured and he didn't waste any time. He unfolded the Sunday paper, took out a pair of brushes and played a swing rhythm on the paper.

'Can you play this?' he said.

Dave shook his head but before the last shake, I had started to play *Guitar Boogie* and two minutes later I was asked to join his group. While Dave admitted that drink had given him the courage to phone, he had also thought that tuition was included. I did my brother a big favour that day. He is now his own boss, running a very successful business and very happy that he couldn't play drums.

Tony had made a date for me to meet the other new recruits to the group in a damp old room behind the 'Ewe and Lamb' pub in Bridge Street. The walls were whitewashed, a single bulb was attached to a dodgy wire hanging out of the ceiling and right across one wall was a mirror, which Tony had placed there to make sure that we all moved together. It was hard to accept at first, but it didn't take long for us to realise just how useful it would be.

I was introduced to the rest of the guys and they certainly were a mixed bunch. John 'Juj' Hopkins was tall and skinny and played the vibraphone, a strange instrument to have in a pop group. Don Ringsell from Dundee was the bass player, who also had a pleasant voice. Last, but not least, was the drummer, Dave Morrow, the son of a local taxi driver. I discovered that Tony, Juj, and Don had been in Singapore together in a band called the Blue Shadows. Tony had decided to buy himself out of the RAF, leave Singapore and return to his father's home in Leighton Buzzard and reform his band, but with a different name for obvious reasons. Tony, along with the other three, had already performed in a show under the name of 'The Knights of the Round Table' and soon realised that the band lacked a guitarist, but I couldn't understand why he wanted another drummer. Dave Morrow, in my opinion, was terrific.

# *The Wing Commander*

Tony's father, Wing Commander Osmond (Rtd), took great interest in the band. When we needed money to buy sound equipment and amplification, he guaranteed a bank loan from the Nat West bank. Of course, it helped that John Morris, the Bank Manager, was his close friend. The Wing Commander was uncertain about the name of the band, which he thought consisted of too many words when it came to advertising on posters and that the size of the print would be small and unreadable from the other side of the road. Then right out of the blue he said, 'Why don't you call yourselves the Barron Knights?' Until his passing day he never knew why he said it.

In his retirement, he took a part-time job as manager of a filling station in Dunstable. Every day a young lorry driver would come in to fill-up and never failed to tell a couple of jokes. The WC took to Tony Avern like a son and suggested that on his delivery trips, maybe he could find the local dance hall and book a show for his son Tony's group, the Barron Knights. This idea was greeted with much enthusiasm by Tony Avern, who was so keen on the idea that he always took his suit along and got changed in the cab before meeting anybody.

So you see, the WC was instrumental in making two very important decisions in the early history of the Barron Knights; choosing the name and finding our manager of twenty-five years. Whenever we rehearsed at 'Whitehayes', their family home, Mrs Osmond would always feed us so well. She was the first person ever to put a curry in front of me. (It was very hot and didn't take long to be behind me!) She used to make a big pot of this curry which lasted for days and tasted better as it got older. Even up until 1986 Mrs Osmond insisted upon someone steering her wheelchair towards one of our shows. She never missed a trick and was always constructive with her criticism. The encouragement that those two gave us was so important and I will always be eternally grateful.

## The First Show

The wheels were now in motion for us to do the first show as the Barron Knights. We had worked very hard for weeks in order to be able to perform two 45 minute 'spots'. It meant repeating a couple of songs, but nevertheless we were eager to go. The music was mainly instrumental and included *Tequila*, *Guitar Boogie* and *Sabre Dance*. The songs were mostly from the hit parade of the day plus a few standards. I loved *Shakin' All Over* because I could show off my playing ability, but hated *Tell Laura I Love Her*, as it was long and boring. *Please Don't Tease* by Cliff Richard was such a good song for its time and included a tricky bit during the guitar solo, which I mastered after a time. I could never understand why Hank Marvin had wanted to play it that way; but thirty years later at his house in Perth, Australia, he admitted that it was a bit of an accident, but they liked the result, so they kept it. Don performed the ballads with his smooth but slightly nasal sound and Tony sang the up-tempo songs. Juj and I didn't have a vocal spot, but we helped out with back-up harmonies.

The Forster Institute, Linslade was to be the venue for our debut show. We advertised in the local rag and I must have told everyone who drew breath. We hung the vocal speakers on the picture rails with meat hooks, miles away from the stage, in order to avoid feed-back. There were three microphones, one each for lead vocal, backing vocal and vibes. Although we had two guitars, there was only one guitar amplifier, but Don had a massive speaker cabinet for his bass. Dressed in our grey Italian-style suits, we were ready.

Tony Avern was in charge of the door and couldn't believe the size of the queue. He had been warned about a couple of trouble-makers, so when it was their turn to pay, he cleverly played a psychological trick. He asked them to walk around the dance hall and keep a check on any trouble. I hastened to explain that Tony was an ex-middle-weight boxer and as he looked every inch the part, it wasn't too difficult to persuade the hard men of Leighton Buzzard to help out. They were so proud to be given the job of bouncers, that we never saw a fight, ever. Although we were nervous and in need of more rehearsal, the show was very well received. The crowd wouldn't let us off stage and so Friday night at the Forster Institute became a regular venue. As I was the only local person in the band, it took time for me to get used to standing on stage in front of all the folks with whom I had grown up.

It was around this time that plain Tony Osmond became Barron Anthony. He changed his name so as to establish the fact that he was the leader and he did an excellent job, carefully choosing the material for the show and deciding how it should be presented . . . With the help of the giant-sized mirror.

We rehearsed three or four nights a week which improved my guitar playing, and I began to tentatively join in the backing vocals. Consequently, Barron suggested that I had a song in the show; his reason being that he wanted the group to appear versatile. So there I was on a Friday night at the Forster Institute, worrying about my debut as a singer. My choice of song was *Dark Town Strutters Ball*, the Joe Brown version, as it had a cheekiness about it that I could handle. I was in a 'shit or bust' situation and as I didn't want to let the boys down I went for it, giving it my all. It definitely stopped all the people dancing, a fact that Barron liked very much. Very soon after that I was asked to learn another song, the Terry Scott children's favourite *My Brother*. It was included in the show for over three years and never failed to stop the crowd dancing. Looking back, it's hard to believe just how effective that song was. Just imagine; the Sixties revolution was just beginning and there I was singing *My Brother* to a dance hall full of Mods and Rockers! *Little Darling* by the Diamonds was also a big favourite and we covered a few other American vocal group records, adding movements in the style made popular by the black groups. Whenever we were working with other groups, it was becoming obvious that we had a unique style of performance. We seemed destined to be a Show group; that would be the direction in which we would go. Wherever we performed, it was our aim to stop the dancing by the second number and keep our audience gathered around the stage. We usually succeeded.

There was one major problem staring us in the face. Although Don could handle the ballads, neither he nor Barron nor I could sing any 'Elvis' or 'Cliff' numbers. We needed a strong vocalist who could adapt from Blues to Soul and Rock'n'Roll. We auditioned Ted West, who was one of my old school friends: there was nobody else around we could think of. Then Tony Avern was keen to bring over one of his friends from

Dunstable . . . enter Richard Eddie Palmer. At the audition he sang every song like Ray Charles, but it was obvious that he had potential. Barron sent him away with the task of learning *Surrender* and *It's Now or Never*. He came back a few days later, word-perfect. His first show was in Rushden, Northampton-shire, with his new name . . . Dickie Demon.

# On The Road at Last

Tony didn't have too much trouble in finding us gigs. Aylesbury Grosvenor, Bletchley, Biggleswade, Bedford, Luton, Chicksands American Air Force base and of course the famous California Ballroom, Dunstable were just a few of the regular dates. The whole of the Bedford area was 'sewn up' by Rocky Rivers, who provided us with many Friday nights at the Conservative Club and, on the odd occasion, the Corn Exchange. In Bill Wyman's book *Stone Alone*, he confesses to having seen us in Aylesbury and blames the Barron Knights for his inspiration to join a pop group.

One night in Biggleswade, we were well-supported by a couple of coach loads from Leighton Buzzard and included in the party were a few of the local heavies, of whom Stan Tyers and Alfie Kempster were the ring-leaders. Unfortunately, some of the Biggleswade boys showed displeasure at our performance, so, in the only way they knew, Stan, Alf and Co. breathed fire and within twenty minutes were being escorted out by what seemed like the whole of the Bedfordshire Constabulary. Thirty-two years later, I met Stan and Alf in Leighton Buzzard and the first thing they reminded me of was that bloody night in Biggleswade. Hooray for fan worship, may it never die!

The most prestigious date in the area was, without doubt, the California Ballroom, where we came across our first serious rivals, Russ Sainty and the Nu Notes. Russ was a good-looking front man with a super voice and the guitarist, Rhet Stoller was the best I'd seen so far. They were like us, a Show group and didn't specialise in one particular style of music, just anything that was in the charts. Whatever they did, they did very well and certainly gave us a 'kick up the bum' to raise our standards! Rhet, who sat down for the whole show, produced a great sound with his Binson echo machine and when he played *Caravan*, the whole of the dance floor was motionless. It must have lasted for ten minutes and so did the applause! Even now, in the Nineties, Russ is still crooning to the girls and whenever we're in the Portsmouth area, he's the first one into the dressing room, showing off his youthful looks . . . The swine!

## *The Coach*

Not only was our act becoming unique, but our transportation was raising a few eyebrows as well. We bought a 27-seater Bedford coach and replaced twenty of the seats with bunk beds. There was no way we could afford hotels of any description, so this was the only option. It looked as dull as a Swiss hotelier, so we set about giving it a 'birthday'. It ended up pillar box red and, as Barron was an excellent artist, he painted the words 'Barron Knights' along the whole length of the coach and on

*Barron, Duke and myself on our bunks inside the coach.*

the back, five cartoons of Knights in Armour, with our individual names under each one. Once, while parking this 'blood transfusion on wheels', an elderly limping car park attendant was heard to say, 'What's this then, a bloody circus?' He wasn't far wrong.

The seven seats remaining were the front ones: the driver's, the two next to the driver and the next pair back that were side-on, which isn't the ideal way to travel two hundred miles. We made a rule that stood for three years; whoever carried Don's massive bass cabinet in and out of the venue had the first choice of front seat. There were more arguments about that front seat than anything else and at one time, Don and Dave even fought for it, but judo helped Dave to win.

## *Peanuts for Fifteen Years*

Rhet Stoller was becoming a thorn in my side. I knew my capabilities and could have easily matched what he was doing, if only I had the equipment that produced those wonderful guitar sounds.

Barron knew what I was craving for, so we both drove over to Luton and bought a Swiss echo box. It made an incredible sound. Now all I needed was a classic guitar piece to make the crowd go barmy. I soon found it in *Peanut Vendor*. I practised to the bones and added the simple trick of playing one string very fast, while sliding my left hand as high as it would go up the frets. It was so effective, I couldn't go wrong and wherever we went, I had to play it at least twice. As soon as the boys sang

'PEANUTS', the crowd just crammed around the stage. At the American Air Force Base, Chicksands in Bedfordshire, we used to do three one-hour spots and the audience were never afraid to shout out their requests.

'Hey Peanuts, play *Peanut Vendor,*' bellowed this ten foot negro. Who was I to disagree? That which made Milwaukee famous, put them in the sort of mood that I never argued with. After the show, Barron, who so wanted all members to have a nickname, decided that from then on I was to be called 'Peanuts', although I wasn't so keen.

With names like Barron, Peanut, Dickie Demon and Juj how could we fail? Poor Don and Dave sounded quite ordinary, but were happy to stay that way.

## North-Bound

Tony Avern was doing an excellent job in securing bookings for us. There were always enough to keep us going, but the suit in the lorry really paid off when we were booked for a show at the Coventry Lacarno.

This was the big time: a big city, a big venue and a big worry! The dance hall was in the middle of this newly-built city and as we couldn't park anywhere near the place, the 'get in' was very awkward. We humped guitars, speakers and amplification along pavements, up four flights of stairs, through corridors and eventually into the hall, where we discovered a revolving stage which took two minutes to complete a turn! When the show began, we were astounded to see so many bee-hive hairstyles and Italian-style suits. We'd never seen so many people in front of us. This show was a real test for us, because for once our regular following were absent but much to our relief, we were so successful that the return bookings went on for a very long time. To go north and conquer was good for our egos, although we knew that there was still a big space above Coventry that was yet to be explored. Robin Eldridge, who was based in Doncaster, was the first Northern agent that we ever worked for and over the next three years we played at venues in Barnsley, Scunthorpe, Rotherham, Mexborough, Thorn and performed the first of many shows at Armthorpe Miners Welfare.

After every show we would always go back to our base, which was the car park outside Doncaster Baths. Every morning, as soon as we were up, we were in the baths and we usually had a swim in the afternoons too. We took our meals in Elvins cafe in the High Street and it wasn't long before the staff were treating us like their own family. Not only did their bilberry pie became a very important part of our diet, but they laundered our shirts for us, while we spent hours working out our new ideas for the show. Our first show in Scunthorpe was at the Baths, where we came across the best band that we'd ever seen, Mike Sager and The Crestas. Their line-up consisted of drums, bass, two guitars and Mike who sang with two girl back-up singers. The guitar-playing was excellent and they produced a fabulous vocal sound, so we were, yet again, being set a high standard to match, as we had been with Russ Sainty many months before. However, it wasn't too long before the Barron Knights had gathered quite a following in Yorkshire.

We had heard so much about the Northern Club scene, especially in the mining areas of Yorkshire and Nottinghamshire, that it was quite a daunting prospect to enter through the doors of such places. Everything you may have heard about them is true. They still have rules that are like Commandments in that they have been written and therefore can never be changed. In these Clubs, it wasn't so much that you were in fear of the audience, but more likely, the compere. He had his little raised box, halfway down the room against the wall, and a microphone, into which he frequently blew, to test its efficiency. That was when we knew it was our turn to face the crowd!

'Can I have the best of order, Lais and Genlmen, comon please, turns are coming on. Now this next lot are from the South. Before you say anything, I met them this afternoon when they were having a practice, and I think they are nice lads and a bloody good troupe. They're not a bad price and the contract's on the notice board for all to see. By the way, Tom Braithwaite died peacefully in his sleep last night; he'd been ill for some time. Here they are then, the Barron Knights!'

Having recovered from uncontrollable fits of the giggles, we proceeded to give them our best! However, in the middle of Duke's romantic ballad, we heard the sound of air blowing into the microphone again.

'Lais and Genlmen, pies are now ready . . . best of order, please.'

Greasborough and Ollerton were two very famous Clubs on the circuit, well before Batley came onto the scene. We used to 'double' them. At 8 pm we would perform a forty minute spot at the first Club and then dash over to the next place for the 10 pm show. We would open every window in the coach so that we could dry out between shifts! It was at Ollerton that we first met the brilliant Norman Collier. As zany in the dressing room as he was on stage, he never knew how to put his act together. One night, he asked me what I thought he should open with. For a laugh, I told him that the chicken impression was my favourite. As his act was introduced, the curtains opened and he was seen squatting on a chair, going 'Cock-a-doodle-doo'. The crowd had no idea what was going on, so consequently Norman spent the next half hour working to what must have seemed

23

like a brick wall! I was partly to blame, but I was still shocked to see him open his act with his finale! A limping, concert secretary paid him, in cash, in front of everyone in the bar. He shouted across the length of the bar to Norman, who was at the opposite end with his well-earned pint, 'Norman, was it thirty or thirty-five?'

Norman just went into hysterical laughter. When we meet up again, on the odd occasion, we always remind one another of those wonderful moments.

Yorkshire people have always given the Barron Knights a very warm reception. They seem to like our sense of humour and we like their hospitality. Clubland in this beautiful part of England is such a unique area to work, but the star of the show will always be the compere, or, as he is better known, the concert secretary! One such person introduced a young lady singer as follows: 'You've all heard of this next female. I don't care what you may have read about her in the Sunday Papers, give the cow a chance! Here she is, Dusty Springfield!'

# The First Change

As there were no two characters alike in our set-up, we found that we could put up with one another's little idiosyncrasies quite well. However, having a moody drummer was very difficult to tolerate because it distracted us from our creative work.

Dave would sulk, disappear, argue for the sake of it and

sometimes did not arrive at rehearsals. Although he was very gentle and kind, he was not one who co-operated with the unwritten rules that help to run a pop group in the smoothest possible way. Unfortunately, Barron had very little choice but to tell Dave that he had to go and it was very sad to see him pack his drums away for the last time.

Dave was replaced by Howie Condor. We found him in Darlington whilst we were on our return trip home from Scotland. When he joined us, he was just sixteen years old, good-looking in a baby-faced kind of way and a very capable drummer. He was quite happy to move to Leighton Buzzard and it took him only a few weeks to settle into a tiny caravan, which he parked next door to the rehearsal rooms, behind the pub. Things began to run smoothly again.

# Scotland

Possibly by means of carrier pigeon, our reputation had reached as far as Elgin in the north of Scotland. Alberto Benicci, an Italian immigrant, ran an agency from the 'Two Red Shoes Café' and in 1961 he asked us to go up to the area for a two week tour.

From Leighton Buzzard we went to Portsmouth; after the show there, we drove overnight to Chesterfield and from there we again drove overnight to Perth, where, having parked the coach at the back of the transport cafe, we tucked into a big breakfast before retiring to our bunks for a good day's sleep. (It was the first time the group had been away from home for more than a couple of days and Mum had packed me a biscuit tin full of paste sandwiches, just in case of an emergency. At 3 am somewhere between Manchester and Glasgow, I had thanked her very much.) Our journey from Perth to Elgin began about 8 pm, when we were all rested, clean and full of egg, beans, chips, bread and butter as well as the compulsory large mug of tea.

Juj was driving and I had been nominated to navigate. It was quite easy really; up the A9 for miles, just after Aviemore take the A95 to Craigellachie and turn left to Elgin. Within twenty minutes I had fallen asleep and I woke up three hours later, when we were just fifty yards before the A95 sign. I said, 'Left here, Juj.'

He mumbled back, 'Good job you stayed awake, I'd have missed it.'

The 'Two Red Shoes Café' became our base and from there we worked in Oban, Inverness, Nairn, Tain, Buckie, Invergordon and Thurso. When we arrived in Invergordon and found that the locals didn't know anything about a show, we ran around every shop, garage and house to let the people know. They were apparently so starved of entertainment, that the result was a full house and we made enough money for the journey to the next show.

That journey was to become the most horrendous twenty-four hours of our career.

After packing the gear back into the coach we headed for Montrose and from there we drove south to Inverness, then east to Aberdeen. Snow had begun to fall and the roads were very slippery. We approached Inverurie around 7.30 am and it was then that the elements beat us! A bus, coming from the opposite direction, kissed our coach and caused a nasty scrape along the side. Luckily there were no injuries, so we swapped addresses and carried on with the journey. Arriving in Montrose about 4 pm, we were in no mood to play music to another load of

Scottish, teenage drunks, as we had done at some recent venues. We found the hall, and fortunately the caretaker lived next door. He answered our knock,

'What do you want, laddie?' The tightly-clipped, Scottish accent frightened us to death. Barron spoke up, 'We're the Barron Knights and we're doing a show here tonight.'

In an even more aggressive tone the caretaker replied, 'I've never heard of ya and there's no show here tonight . . .' Slam! We were stunned into silence. Our funds were low and so the only answer was to ring Mr Benicci in Elgin. He listened to our story, then calmly said, 'Oh! didn't I tell you lads, you have the night off.' Then added, 'Don't forget that you're in Elgin tomorrow!'

We had passed through Elgin at about 3 am that morning!

We later discovered that following us around on that particular tour was a group from Liverpool, with such a strange name . . . The Beatles!

## *Butch for the Second Time*

Once the payments for the bank loan had been met, we began to draw a pound or two from the remainder of the funds. My guitar was a white, semi-acoustic Hoya, but now solid guitars were the things to have, so off I pranced down to Charing Cross Road, where Jim Burns had the best selection. His shop was like an Aladdin's Cave. Hundreds of guitars were hanging around the walls, with wires and amps all over the floor. I ended up by buying a 'Fenton Weil' and couldn't wait to get the beautiful beast on stage. I spent many a Saturday morning at

Jim Burns's shop and quite often saw Jimmy Page and Eric Clapton demonstrating their skills. I remember thinking . . . Blimey, I've got plenty of practising ahead of me!

On one of those particular days, I had rather a pleasant surprise; while I was sitting in the shop playing and posing, without any warning, in walked Butch. We had so much to catch up on, that we decided to spend the day together. I discovered later that he'd just broken up from a very strong relationship with which he'd been involved for a long time and he was on a 'downer', so to talk about things was the best thing for him. We walked through Trafalgar Square to Westminster Bridge and hopped onto a sightseeing River Thames cruiser going to the Tower and back, where we had a good laugh at the guy on the microphone who described the historic buildings along the way, and then asked for a tip!

In a tiny cafe in the Strand, I described what had happened to me since he had left Leighton Buzzard. He hung onto my every word and I knew he would have given anything to have been in the band. The thought of rocking and rolling with pay was very attractive and I would have moved mountains to take him back on the train with me and into the rehearsal room.

As we said our goodbye's, I wasn't at all confident that I'd done a very good job of cheering him up at all.

## *The Second Change*

Tony Avern was proving himself to be a rare breed; that is, a manager/agent who was not just interested in a percentage deal, but wanted to be an equal partner. Spreading his wings, he began to mix with the London agents and he found out that it was tough and competitive, but loved every minute of it. He discovered that they all knew about the Barron Knights, therefore, selling us wasn't too much of a problem. As he gradually learned of all the pit-falls, he soon became well-respected. *Our* job was to make sure he always had a good product to sell.

The toughest of all the agents was Roy Tempest, but in a short space of time, he became like a baby sparrow in the palm of Tony's hands. Between the two of them they certainly found us plenty of gigs.

One night, while we were in the middle of rehearsals, Tony arrived to tell us that we had been offered a two-week stint at the Top Ten Club in Hamburg. Apart from the fact that the money we were being offered was very good, this booking suggested something far more significant. Our diary was filling up all the time, which meant that to be wholly committed to the group *and* hold down a day job was almost impossible.

To turn professional was the ambition of us all, or so we thought! Juj wasn't so sure. He had a good job and as he wasn't too far away from being a married man, it didn't take long for him to make the decision to leave. We were all extremely sad, because not only was he a good bloke but he was the only proper musician amongst us.

We needed a replacement and quickly. Vibraphone players were hard to come by, but did we really want another one? It was a mutual decision that we should recruit another guitarist; someone I could 'bounce off'; someone to put the group 'in vogue'. I didn't have to think twice. Butch!

I knew he was going to be home at the weekend, so I biked over to Pitstone to tell him the story and he agreed to come to the next rehearsal and meet the boys. I'd spoken to Barron about Butch and he agreed to audition him, but he said there was someone else he had in mind who he'd seen playing in the

'Peacock' pub in Leighton Buzzard. He was a great guitarist but Barron didn't know his name. I tried to explain to Barron that no one would be better than Butch and furthermore, Juj's suit would fit, because Butch was another long streak of nothing.

Howie ambled in from his caravan, Dickie arrived on his motorbike and Don, Barron and myself were going through a few things. I was quite nervous for Butch. This was his big night. Half an hour later, he walked in.

'Farting Moses,' Barron yelled, 'I've been trying to contact you.' With a big grin Butch drawled back, 'Well dang me, here ah am.'

Unbeknown to Barron and myself, we had been boasting to one another about the same guy and we were both very relieved at the outcome. Needless to say, rehearsals were cut short and we spent the rest of the evening celebrating in the 'Ewe and Lamb'.

Although Veronica, my girlfriend of two years, had given me all the encouragement I needed, she wasn't too keen on the idea of me sailing off to Germany for two weeks. Our's was a serious relationship, but it was always a struggle just to have a night together. Fortunately, she understood the situation and on many occasions would just sit in the rehearsal room and listen to our music.

On the 30th September, 1962, we left for Hamburg. We caught the ferry to Ostend where Peter Echorn, the manager of the 'Top Ten Club', was waiting for us. He had a VW Combi and that was to accommodate the five of us, plus our guitars and cases. We sat like sardines for eight hours, with one stop for a pee and one stop for Peter to take a 'keep me awake' pill and at around breakfast time, we arrived in the Reeperbahn in Hamburg and were very grateful to be walking again!

Never having been out of England before, I didn't know what to expect, but was shocked when before I'd even unloaded my suitcase, we witnessed these two men screaming at one another. First one took off at a rate of knots, then the other pulled out a gun and fired at the runner. *We* ran into the Club, wondering just what we were in for during the next couple of weeks. After a quick look at our work place, we moved into the hotel next door for a good sleep. Like most buildings in the whole street, our hotel was used for the 'ladies of the night', which answered the question why there were so many young women everywhere. The whole scene was a bit scary but we soon got used to it and carried on with the job of making music.

We were to perform alternate hours for four hours, while the other slots were shared with another English band called The Flintstones. The first time that I ever saw a bass guitar played with the fingers, it was played by Rupert of the Flintstones. He was brilliant, but sadly died not long after the Hamburg trip. Terry Slater, the guitarist, went on to become head of A&R at EMI and later managed the group 'Ah Ha'. The other venue in town that booked English bands was called the 'Star Club'. Little Richard, the Everley Brothers and a few other big American acts were advertised on the poster outside, but inside a young Gerry and the Pacemakers were performing, with the help of the Searchers. Two hundred yards up the street from the 'Top Ten Club' was a cafe with the unforgettable name of the 'Mambo Shanki'. We couldn't afford to eat there every day, but twice a week we congregated there with the Liverpool bands. All they used to talk about was Soul and Rhythm and Blues, while we talked about the price of sending a postcard home, or did we have enough money for goulash and boiled potatoes!

Butch was petrified about his début with the Barron Knights. At rehearsals, he smoked about forty cigarettes and decided he couldn't go through with it, if it meant him having to play guitar and sing. As he was so lacking in confidence, we decided to just let him stand there and play tambourine but within days, he was into the swing of things and difficult to hold back.

31

Our time in Hamburg wasn't the easiest two weeks, but it served its purpose by easing Butch into the show. Our act was full of chart songs, such as, *I Remember You*, *Speedy Gonzales*, *A Picture Of You*, *Sealed With A Kiss*, *Things*, *Tower Of Strength*, *Let There Be Drums*, and the show-stopper, *Blue Moon*. I managed to make *Peanut Vendor* last about six minutes! There was a sigh of relief when those two weeks came to an end.

On the way home, we 'whipped' through Customs with no problem at all, but Gerry Marsden wasn't so fortunate. When asked if he had anything to declare, Gerry, in his broad Scouse accent said, 'Yes, the Crown Jewels!' The Customs Officers held him for six hours, while they stripped and searched the whole band, took the wheels off the van and made sure that the next time he went through Customs, he behaved himself.

# The Third Change

Howie began to act strangely. He was constantly ill and found it difficult to cope with the pressures involved in trying to make it in the pop world. We were doing so many shows, the travelling was exhausting to say the least and we must have been wearing a groove in the A1 and A5. He eventually had a nervous breakdown and the doctor advised us to replace him, as he didn't feel that Howie had the strength to cope with our punishing schedules.

We had twenty-four hours in which to find a new drummer before the next show at the Top Rank in Reading and we didn't even *know* another drummer, so we telephoned Tony

Holly the sax player from the Flintstones. Fortunately, he knew of someone who had just finished working on a cruise ship and was looking for a job. We were very relieved when Dave Ballinger arrived to help us out, even though we knew it was only temporary. After Dave had been introduced to the strange names of Barron, Don, Peanuts, Duke, and Butch, he said, 'What am I joining, a bloody circus?' Twice in two years we'd been called that!

He had three hours to learn the act. It was an impossible task, but the audience didn't know any different and as usual, we lived to fight another day.

Although Dave had to go back to his job on the ships, he kindly stayed for a few more weeks, until we had found a permanent replacement. (More bloody rehearsals.) Then, from Hitchin, came Sharky, our fourth drummer in two years.

## *The Fourth Change*

Sharky had been in a local band called the Tartans. He was an Aberdonian and, like many Scots musicians, was very keen on jazz. As Don came from Dundee they struck up a good friendship, but in the early part of 1963, I began to notice that the fun seemed to be going out of the band. The two Scots lads would always go one way and we four went the other.

We were beginning to get so busy that the only time I could see my girlfriend, Veronica, was at lunchtimes. I used to meet her outside the hairdressers where she worked, bike to her home and fall asleep while she ate her lunch. Her mother wasn't particularly impressed with my energy level, but she knew that her daughter was completely aware of the situation!

After every show in the London area, we used to stop on the way home at the transport cafe at Markyate. It was always full of twenty-stone lorry drivers and it seemed wise to make sure that they were served first! The six of us, plus Tony, were all sitting around one table, when we bet him a pound that he wouldn't drink his mug of tea, even after we had mixed it with anything that was lying around. Like a fool he agreed. Daddie's sauce, HP sauce, salt, pepper, mustard and just for good measure a cigarette butt or two, all went into the tea. It was lightly stirred and away he went! He drank it as quickly as Oliver Reed and ran outside with the speed of Linford Christie. Up came the whole mugful. It had been snowing very heavily for twenty-four hours and he managed to choose the deepest drift in which to exhibit his artwork! When he'd been outside for more than ten minutes, we began to worry and decided to check on his whereabouts. We found him digging in the drift with his bare hands: he looked awful and managed to mumble,

'It's alright for you lot to laugh, but I've lost me bleedin' false teeth.' We eventually found them thank goodness, but his Popeye impression was great.

Howie wanted his job back. Knowing what punishing schedules were ahead, we couldn't risk a repeat of the problems, although he was a better drummer than Sharky. Because of our refusal, he sued us for 'wrongful dismissal': he didn't stand a chance because we had based our actions upon medical advice.

The case of 'Barron Knights *versus* Howie Condor' is now used as the precedent for wrongful dismissal cases in any court of law using British justice.

*The new band 1963. L. to R. Sharky, Barron, Don, Butch, me and Dickie Demon seated.*

# 'If You Gotta Make A Fool Of Somebody'

In March, 1963 we were asked to appear on a BBC TV tea-time show called *Lets Go*, which was designed to show off new talent. We knew exactly which song we would perform. One of the most outstanding routines in our show at the time was *If You Gotta Make A Fool Of Somebody*, in which we used to sway from side to side and lift our legs up and down. Also on that same show was a group from Manchester called Freddie and the Dreamers and their offering was *We Wear Short Shorts*.

Within weeks, Freddie, having copied our whole routine, was signed up by EMI and by June, he and the Dreamers were not only number three in the charts with *If You Gotta Make A Fool Of Somebody* but also performing our movements, step for step. We met him a few weeks later, at a Sunday concert in Great Yarmouth, when he opened our dressing room door and said, 'Get the hatchets out, lads.' So who were the fools?

My Dad was very tearful when he saw our first TV appearance. He knew then that he was losing his battle against lung cancer and wouldn't be around to see any future successes. He christened himself 'One Lung the Chinaman': he had humour until the end.

# The First Single

By mid 1963, we had covered most of the big dance halls in England and Scotland and we were doing capacity business everywhere, even without the magic hit record. All the Mecca and Top Rank ballrooms were booming and the Mods had become the backbone of the Swinging Sixties.

We were setting up our sound system one afternoon at the Top Rank, Bradford, when we were approached by a lady with a little girl. The girl's name was Pauline and she wanted us to give her a chance to sing in front of the crowd that night. She stood at the microphone and belted out the Skeeter Davis hit *End of the World*. She had a very mature voice for such a young person and that night she had won the crowd over even before she'd finished the first verse.

Pauline arrived in London a couple of years later, changed her name to Kiki Dee and became one of the most respected female vocalists this country has ever produced. She should have been a world-wide recording star but the choice of material for her singles was not of the consistently high standard that she required.

Tony managed to fix a session with Tony Hatch at Pye records and it turned out to be a most embarrassing afternoon. When we had finished the first song he said, 'At what speed would you like it; the one you started with or the one you ended up with?' We left Cumberland Place with our chins on the pavement. A week later, we were five hundred yards down the road at Philips Fontana, recording the first song I had ever written, *Lets Face It*. I couldn't wait to see our name on that round piece of plastic and seeing my own as the writer, gave me the incentive I needed to write many more songs.

Sadly, it was a 'miss'. It didn't quite have the strength to reach the charts but most people thought the flip-side, *Never Miss Chris*, could have done much better.

One of our biggest problems was the fact that we were developing into a comedy band on stage, yet at the same time, trying to be 'straight' on record. Because of our reputation, we were signed up by an independent producer called Denis Preston, who owned Lansdowne Studios off Ladbroke Grove. His 'big gun' was Acker Bilk and *Stranger On The Shore* had netted him a fortune in 1961. Again, we recorded one of my songs, but *Joanne* was not to be the chart success for which we were so desperately hoping. However, Denis was keen to keep us on and told us not to rush things. Our knowledge of public image was nil and although our act was improving every day, where could we go to find a song to fit the Barron Knights?

It was June 1963 when we started our tour of the seaside resorts. We kicked off at Dreamland, the massive ballroom in Margate. The mods arrived in their thousands and we soon found out why: our support group for the night was a bunch of lads with the longest hair I'd ever seen and their names were the Rolling Stones. Mick Jagger played a mean harmonica, while Bill Wyman chewed gum and pointed his bass to the ceiling. As the girls all screamed, we stood and watched in amazement and slowly began to learn about image and its effect on the public.

Every Sunday, throughout the summer, we were at the Brittania Pier, Great Yarmouth, and to say that the bill was a crowd puller was an understatement: Billy Fury, Joe Brown, Dickie Pride, Vince Eager, Mike Preston, Tommy Bruce and of course, Freddie and his Dreamers. We opened the show and then became the backing band for Dickie, Vince and Mike. Once again we saw girls go berserk: this time at Billy Fury and they really did take their knickers off and throw them on stage. So it *was* true what the papers printed. But it was tough watching Freddie sing *If You Gotta Make a Fool Of Somebody*.

# Brian Epstein

In 1962, every city in the country was over-run with pop groups. While Birmingham and Manchester had their fair share, all we heard about was the 'Mersey Sound'. When we were in Scotland, we'd heard about the Beatles and according to the NME, Liverpool was the only place to be. Runcorn and Widnes were as close as we could get and our sense of humour was very well received, considering that Liverpudlians are as sharp as razors. After the Widnes show, a visitor entered the dressing room. He was dressed too smartly for the occasion but his manner was as immaculate as his suit.

'I'm Brian Epstein and I manage the Beatles. I'd like to know where you get your vocal sound equipment from?'

He spoke as if the Beatles were already big stars and we found out later that they were, in Liverpool. He complimented us on our slick performance and we answered his question. We didn't see him again for about a year, but when we did, how important it was!

Doncaster and Sheffield were also producing good bands in those days. Shane Fenton and the Fentones, along with Dave Berry and the Cruisers, all had the ingredients for success and we always shared the bill with them at Barnsley and Rotherham Baths.

We were now covering all areas of the country. Southampton Pier became a big venue, also Kingston Jazz Cellar, The Breaks, Hatfield and Hitchin Hermitage. On the posters outside these places, there were always the same names printed: Cliff Bennett and the Rebel Rousers, Screaming Lord Sutch and the Savages, Rory Storm and Barry James and the Strangers. One thing was certain, they had all heard of the Beatles: nothing was going to stop *them* becoming big stars.

# *Ireland*

In the autumn, we caught the ferry from Holyhead to Dublin for the first of our many Irish tours and this one, without doubt, must be called Butch's tour.

The first show was in Bray. The dance hall was by the sea and unloading the gear was an exercise more fitting to a trained Marine Commando; it was bitterly cold and pouring with rain. In the few weeks that Butch had been in the band, he was slowly developing his own brand of humour. I like to describe it as 'gently mad'. *Sally*, the old Gracie Fields hit, was his first solo performance. We played it in a swing rhythm and during the intro he had his back to the audience and girated his hips as Elvis did.

As he sang the opening word, he spun around to face the audience, who all howled with laughter and we thought, wow! this is going to be great. By the second verse we had found out why: his fly zip was wide open revealing his bright red underpants and his face quickly went the same shade. Since that show, every night before the curtains open, Butch will be heard to say, 'Check your flies, lads.'

We followed on to Cork, Limerick and Dundalk, before catching the night ferry back to Holyhead and straight into a force 9 gale. I hope I never experience seas like that again. The waves tossed us about like an empty plastic bottle and looking up I saw the sea and looking down I saw the sky. All the passengers were throwing up, except for one . . . Butch. He was knocking back the whisky and eating beans on toast, while the rest of us were wanting to die and join the cod! I was feeling so bad that if someone had thrown me overboard, I would have thanked them as I hit the water.

Once we had docked at Holyhead, we gathered our suitcases and equipment together in a pile. Suddenly there was a mighty crash! Another passenger had accidently knocked the Binsen echo machine to the floor, smashing it to bits. Butch turned around to the culprit and said, 'You stupid bastard, can't you watch what you're bloody well doing?'

'God forgive me, I am so sorry,' the man replied, as he turned around to reveal himself as a black priest!

After such a dreadful crossing, the journey back to Leighton Buzzard was awful. Not even Sketchley's could remove the smell from my treasured Ivy League jacket.

## The Beatles Show

1963 was the year that began the Sixties' reputation. The Mersey Sound was booming and the Beatles were on their fourth hit. Many bands with whom we had worked were having hit records, while we were still lagging behind. The only thing we had going for us was our reputation.

After the stint at Great Yarmouth and the Irish tour we still hadn't a clue about what sort of song to record. Then, out of the blue, Brian Epstein rang Tony and asked if we would support the Beatles on their Christmas Show. Since they were now the world's hottest property and had the choice of the whole business, this was a tremendous boost to our egos.

The show was to run from the 24th December to the 11th January at the Finsbury Park Astoria, London. We also did two preview shows, one at the Alhambra, Bradford, and the other at the Liverpool Empire. The line-up for the show consisted of Billy J. Kramer and the Dakotas, Rolf Harris, The Fourmost, Tommy Quickly and Cilla Black. We had to back Cilla and Rolf. As we arrived in Bradford for rehearsals, we found the theatre completely surrounded by thousands of screaming girls, hysterical and totally uncontrollable.

The first part of the show was strange. The Fab Four opened with a sketch performed in semi-darkness, except for the strobe lighting. It ended with a complete blackout for about ten seconds and then we appeared to do our spot. The sketch was a complete waste of time really, because the sound system couldn't compete with three thousand screaming kids. They were still screaming at the end of our last song. We sang three, Mel Torme's *I'm Coming Home Baby*, *You Don't Have To Be A Baby To Cry* and *Little Darling* but if we had performed the Prelude from Bizet's *Carmen*, I'm sure that no one in the audience would have noticed.

Rolf came on to the stage riding a scooter and sang *Tie Me Kangaroo Down Sport*, *Sun Arise* and *I've Lost My Mummy* and he then introduced Cilla, who always complained that our backing was too loud, but fold-back speakers hadn't been thought of at the time. By the time the Beatles came on again, the crowd had surged forward and the kids in the front were getting crushed, but they didn't seem to mind as long as they got a close-up of their idols. The stage was showered with jelly babies and the music was completely overpowered by the screaming, which rose to such a pitch when Paul sang *Til There Was You*, that even a Highland Terrier could have heard it in Inverness.

After the show in Bradford, we decided to drive overnight to Liverpool to ensure that we were in the theatre *before* the crowds started gathering. Rolf had the same idea, so he asked for a lift. We willingly obliged and also offered a bed for the night in our mobile home. At about 3 am, we arrived outside the Liverpool Empire, but Five Knights and Rolf were disturbed around 8 am by hundreds of screaming kids, all singing *Please Please Me*.

The show at Finsbury Park was much more spectacular. Peter Yolland the producer had only a day and a night to put the show together and although he kept us there all through the night on the Monday, by the time the show opened we were still in a pickle. He had special staging made for us, while our amplifiers were hidden beneath our feet. The whole thing moved forward and so consequently, our guitar leads were in tatters as soon as the operation was put into motion. In addition, our sound was muffled by the boxes that the amplifiers were in. But, who were we to argue?

To stand at the side of the stage every night watching Lennon sing *Twist and Shout* was an indescribable experience. The Beatles closed their show with *I Wanna Hold Your Hand*, which had just made Number 1 in the American charts and in the following January, the Fab Four crossed the Atlantic for three appearances on the Ed Sullivan show.

Cilla became a wonderful seamstress in those two weeks. Our uniform consisted of maroon bolero suits and my trousers were very tight with the result that I could never complete a whole show without the dreaded split! Every night I knocked on her door and she was always there with her needle and thread, while Bobby, her future husband, made sure the trousers were back in our dressing room before the next show.

On the closing Saturday night, Paul came into our dressing room and introduced us to a mate of his who had a Beatle hair cut and was to become a star in the next twenty four hours.

Sunday night at the London Palladium had discovered Jimmy Tarbuck!

Being involved in such an historic show, it was unfortunate for the Barron Knights that there was such a bad atmosphere between them. Don and Sharky were giving us a hard time and were never around when they were needed. Their girlfriends had the better of them and they showed no interest in the future of the band. The final showdown came during a show in Corby. Don, Barron and myself were all around one microphone doing the 'oohs' and 'aahs', when a tiny piece of spit landed on Don. It's something that happens all the time in such situations but on this occasion he stopped singing his part and spat right into my face. I was on the verge of walking off stage, but knew that Barron would never have forgiven me. I've always had a very short fuse and how I stopped myself from giving him permanent brain damage that day will always remain a mystery. We had twenty minutes of the show still left to do; enough time to assess how to confront Don and how the consequences would affect the group. Considering the problems that the two Scots boys had given all of us, I made a calculated guess that the majority would be on my side.

I didn't beat about the bush! As soon as we were all in the dressing room, I turned to Barron and said, 'It's either him or me; make your mind up quickly.'

## The Fifth Change

At the meeting the next day, it was decided that Don had to go and, as we expected, Sharky said the predictable 'If he goes, I go.'

The four of us who remained were quite looking forward to the next few weeks of the 'new look' Barron Knights. Barron had decided to take up the bass, while we contacted Dave Ballinger, who agreed to rejoin us and within a week we performed the first show at the Guildhall, Southampton.

We were dreadful!

While Barron worked extremely hard on his bass playing, the rest of us were coming up with fresh ideas for the show. We improved very quickly, but it was a case of having to, because we had some big shows booked in the second half of January, 1964. On the 19th, we were at the Coventry Theatre with the Stones, Ronnettes, Freddie and the Dreamers and the Quiet Five and this time our new line-up proved very successful. On the 26th, we hit De Montfort Hall, Leicester with the same show and while we took the crowd by storm, Freddie and the Stones were arguing about who should be top of the bill.

On the 31st January, we appeared on 'Ready Steady Go', our second TV show. Denis Preston had decided to release *Peanut Butter*, which we'd recorded very hastily and it sounded as if we had: the performance was embarrassing to say the least. All the other acts were singing their hits; there were Gerry and the Pacemakers, Cilla, Brian Poole and the Tremeloes and the Merseybeats, yet the high spot of the show for us was an interview with Keith Fordyce. To make matters worse, the very next day, while unloading our equipment at a dance hall in March, Cambridgeshire, we realised that Butch's guitar had been left at the 'Ready Steady Go' studios in London!

Not the best couple of days for us. But a few weeks earlier, Butch had given me a Christmas present that was to hold the key to our future success.

# The Big Idea

My first major possession had been a Pye black box stereo record player. It took up a big space in Mum's lounge and wasn't the most attractive piece of furniture, but because of her love of music, she was pleased to hear it shaking the walls! My first long playing record was by the Ted Heath Band, but the one I wore out, by playing over and over again, was the Les Paul and Mary Ford LP. I learned the solo to *How High The Moon* by playing it at slow speed, which cost me a fortune in new needles.

Butch knew all about my stereo and bought me a Four Preps LP. It was a very thoughtful present and after I'd played it a thousand times, I spotted an idea that so suited our show; I began to rewrite it to suit the British audiences. We could have used almost every track on the LP for our show, but a track entitled *The Big Draft* was the one that had all the ingredients of a great stage routine. What the Four Preps had done was to change the lyrics of the hits of the day and substitute a story about the groups and singers being drafted to join the Forces. Each song was linked by a short verse, which explained each little story. The key to it all was that they had chosen the songs that everybody knew so well.

My first task was to choose a selection of big British hits. *You Were Made For Me* by Freddie and the Dreamers was my first choice for a lyric change.

I wrote the first things that were coming into my head and Mum's kitchen table became covered with a mass of little bits of paper, all of them full of ideas for the boys to hear. As soon as they heard the basic story, it was a case of heads down and brains working overtime. We sat in 'Whitehayes' for four or five days and structured it both musically and lyrically and the result was an epic that lasted about ten minutes which we entitled *Call Up The Groups*. We had not only changed the lyrics of ten hit songs, but had come up with a routine that was to change our whole lives.

On the 14th February, 1964, we performed our first version of *Call Up The Groups* at the prestigiously named Bagington Aero Club on the outskirts of Coventry. The moment we started this new routine, the crowd looked on in amazement. Their reaction was phenomenal. When we went into a send-up of the Rolling Stones, singing new words to *I Wanna Be Your Man*, they went absolutely bananas!

With the constant publicity about their scruffy looks, plus an enormous amount of effort on our part to copy their movements, we couldn't fail. Barron pointed his bass to the sky and chewed like Bill Wyman, Butch was a wonderful Brian Jones and I played the bandy, swaying Keith Richard. With his name recently changed from Dickie Demon to Duke D'mond, he was the key to it all with his wonderful impersonation of Mick Jagger. We had never experienced such a reaction from an audience. They insisted that we did the whole thing again and they laughed just as hard the second time around! The crowd went wild yet again the following night, when we were at the Hermitage Ballroom, Hitchin.

We had just signed to the Les Perrin publicity agency. He handled the Stones and had predicted a big future for us, but we were still waiting for the big break. After Tony had 'phoned to tell him of this wonderful routine we had written and how well it was going on our live shows, he sent his assistant, David Block, to our next show, which was at the California Ballroom, Dunstable, where we were supporting Dusty Springfield and her group the Echoes with John Paul Jones on the bass. David was amazed at the reaction to *Call Up The Groups*. He came into the dressing room after the show and told us that we had to record it.

'It's a hit,' he said. It hadn't even entered our heads to go into the recording studio with it. Why not?

# Recording 'Call Up The Groups'

On 25th February, 1964, we entered Lansdowne Studios to record *Call Up The Groups*. Dave Heelis, the engineer, set up two microphones, one for the lead vocal and the other for the backing voices. To give him a rough idea of what to expect, we ran through the whole ten minute routine and when we had finished, we heard his voice over the talk-back saying, 'What the hell am I supposed to do with that?'

He had only ever recorded the normal three-minute song from start to finish, not a medley of about twenty bits with different singers, different tempos and volume changes during mid-song! It was like *Ben Hur*, an epic out of all proportion and the whole thing had to be finished by 6 pm. Dave, a genius with the knobs and buttons, only had a four-track machine, so we sat down with him and planned the whole operation. He wrote it all down on paper, then back into the studio we went. During the Dave Clarke *Bits And Pieces* section of the recording, we had difficulty in re-creating the stamping sound for our *Boots And Blisters* routine. No problem for Mr Heelis; he produced a big plank of wood, we marched on it and created the same effect. He admitted later that Dave Clarke had recorded the song at Landsdowne and had used exactly the same piece of wood to make the sound that we were trying to copy.

When six o'clock arrived, we were physically and mentally drained but *Call Up The Groups* was finished and ready to be released, or so we thought. Denis Preston came down from his office, eager to hear our latest offering about which we were all so excited.

'It's very good boys, but you need to make it sound as though you've performed it in front of an audience.'

Denis was well known as a brandy drinker and we thought perhaps he'd had a few too many, but he was quite serious.

'Come back tomorrow and bring your wives, girlfriends, brothers and sisters and we'll give them some wine, play the track and dub their reaction onto a spare track.' We were confused to say the least, but we did as he said and the results were terrific. His theory was that when you hear people laugh, you laugh along with them and how true we found that to be!

He then hit us with another body-blow.

'Of course, before we release the record, you must get written permission from the publishers to say that they agree to the new lyrics of all the songs.'

At first we thought that he was joking, but sure enough, we spent the next few months wearing down our shoe leather around the West End, pleading with the publishers to allow us to release our 'sure-fire' hit. They gave us a hard time and our first round of meetings was very unsuccessful. The idea of hit records being ridiculed was most unpopular and as we found so little co-operation, it seemed to be a hopeless case and the boys were ready to give up. However, I persuaded Tony to persevere. We pestered the publishers so much that we became friends and eventually we were successful with

Keith Prowse and Ardmore and Beechwood. Our biggest stumbling block was Dick James, the Beatles' publisher. We had used *Twist And Shout* for the Beatles' spoof, for which Sherwin Music had given us the green light, but our new version of *I Wanna Be Your Man* was a Lennon and Mc-Cartney song and very precious. He was adamant that in no way were we ever to change the lyrics to a Beatles song.

After about a month of bowing and scraping, we had secured permission for all the songs and links, even from the American Publishers, but there was still no co-operation from Dick James. Then we had one 'last ditch' attempt. Tony Avern and I went to Advision Studios, where we cut two acetates, one of which was posted to Brian Epstein at NEMS and the other I delivered to Dick James' office. First he listened, then he laughed and then he shook his head. We pleaded with him to change his mind, explaining our little friendship with John and Paul. Within twenty minutes, we had persuaded him to write to Brian Epstein.

That was the 10th April, 1964; the day I became engaged to Veronica, the day I passed my driving test and the day I celebrated my 21st birthday (not to mention receiving the letter of confirmation that the Leighton Buzzard Council had agreed to a first mortgage of £2500).

It had to be a lucky day!

On the 15th April, Dick James received the following letter:

15th.April, 1964.

BE/DV.

Dick James, Esq.,
Dick James Music Ltd.,
Suite Two,
132, Charing Cross Road,

LONDON,WC2.

Dear Dick,

Thank you very much for your letter in connection with the
Barron Knights, and also for sending the disc.  I have now had an
opportunity to listen to same, and in fact played it to John Lennon,
(I believe Paul and one of the others had already heard it.).  I
must say that I think that it is a most entertaining and well produced
recording, and one that the Boys and I would have no objection to
seeing become a commercial success.

I appreciate, however, the comments contained in your letter, and
respect same.  But, I would like to put on record, and would really
be obliged if you would please advise those concerned that so far
as the BEATLES and I are concerned we have no objections to the
recording whatsoever.  In fact we would go further and congratulate
the Barron Knights on the recording which we all enjoyed tremendously.

All good wishes.

Yours sincerely,


Brian Epstein.


It was obvious that the Beatles and Brian Epstein were very
much in favour of what we were doing and didn't regard their
particular song as sacred. We jumped for joy and went in search
of a record deal.

I was so excited and relieved, I had a belated birthday party the following day, but it had to be a lunchtime session, because we needed to be in Coventry in the evening. We celebrated in the Golden Bell, Church Square, Leighton Buzzard, where I decided to get drunk and that took no time at all. I remember very little about it, but I've been told by Butch and reminded by most of the locals,that they laid me across the bonnet of Duke's car and drove up and down the High Street, while I shouted up to the window of the hairdressers' shop where Veronica worked, 'I love you!'

The local copper stopped the car and asked Duke, who was also well plastered, if I was alright. Duke nearly said, 'Yes osifer, it's' (belch) 'his birfday.'

That evening, at the Coventry Police Social Club, all I can remember is repeating to Butch,

'How am I doing?'

I haven't a clue what his answer was and he's never volunteered to tell me!

# 'Call Up The Groups' Released

Decca, aided and abetted by Dick Rowe, are famous throughout the world for turning down the Beatles. In April 1964, they added the Barron Knights to their list and they were in good company, because Pye saw no future in such an unusual idea either.

We had two big shows coming up and we couldn't wait to hear the reaction to our future hit. On the 24th May, we were in Coventry again, with the Stones, Julie Grant, Chimes, Overlanders, and the Caravelles. Wembley Arena, on the 31st May, was the next venue, with the Stones once again and Adam Faith, Hollies, Merseybeats, Undertakers, Eden Kane and with David Jacobs acting as compere. The response we received was quite astounding, even though the crowds had never seen anything like it before. Les Perrin, the Stones' publicist, came backstage at Wembley to tell us that he'd heard *Call Up The Groups* and he advised us to go back into the studio and shorten the recording to three take-offs per side.

The magic touch of Dave Heelis made it into a potentially massive hit, ready for release.

Because the Shadows were on the EMI Columbia label, I'd always imagined that it was the best and nothing else would do for the Barron Knights. When we were asked to go to Manchester Square, for a photo session down in the EMI basement, I really felt as though a lead weight had been removed from around my neck.

However, the music press reviews were not too favourable: 'No chance of hit parade success, but a good party record,' said the NME.

No review had anything particularly bad to say, but on the other hand none had anything exciting to say, either.

By the official release date, 7th July, Denis Preston together with EMI were very confident that it would make the charts. The 'pluggers' had performed a miracle. They had arranged for it to be played as a request on *Family Favourites* on the following Sunday and I ran around the town and told just about everybody I saw, regardless of whether I knew them or not.

We were all gathered around the radio that day when Jean Metcalfe introduced our record and even though we knew them all backwards, we laughed at every line. There was no way that it could 'miss'. That one broadcast had made so much impact because, as there were no independent stations at the time, the programme was the only one to listen to.

We were at the Town Hall, Bath on the following Friday, the day that the chart positions were announced and had unloaded the gear and were setting the stage, when I heard a 'phone ring. Could that be Tony with some good news? Like a bloodhound I searched and found the 'phone inside the main entrance. As I picked it up, I had goose pimples.

'Hello.'

'Pete, tell the boys you're number 28 in the NME charts.'

I think I was halfway down the hallway before he put the phone down. Within five minutes, the only thing we were concerned with was what number would it be next week? We all remained very calm about the whole thing and it wasn't until I arrived home and told Mum and Veronica that I really appreciated what had happened.

Although I didn't arrive home from Bath until 3 am, I was up very early that Saturday morning and drove my Renault Dauphine to Veronica's hairdressing shop in order to catch her before the customers began to arrive. We discussed the fact that my £500 overdraft was no longer a problem and maybe moving to a bigger house when we married and going somewhere exotic for our honeymoon. Suddenly the patterns of our lives and thoughts were changing.

There was such an air of excitement everywhere. Every paper and magazine seemed to want photos and interviews and all the folks up the street were discussing whether they had heard the record or not. During that first weekend we sold 30,000 copies!

The following Tuesday, we were at Luton Airport standing on the aircraft steps in front of half a dozen photographers. We were en route to Jersey and I was quite sad to leave all the excitement behind, even for a few days.

*The day we entered the NME top 30 for the first time, July 1964. Flying to Guernsey from Luton Airport.*

55

Perks were something new to us! We were driven around the island, taken out for dinner and it was even arranged that we should have two hours to ourselves at the go-cart track. When the BBC rang the next morning and said that they wanted us to appear on 'Top of The Pops', we had to refuse, as flying to Manchester and back wouldn't allow us to be back in time to do our live show. Two hours later, we were flying north in a six-seater Aztec, which had been hired by 'Auntie'. We recorded the show in the afternoon, flew back to Jersey, watched the show on TV and then went off to Springfield Hall to perform at 10 pm.

The next few weeks were spent in and out of London for interviews and photo calls and recording for Brian Matthews' 'Saturday Club'. We found a slightly different attitude towards us at 'Ready Steady Go' the second time around, with the rest of the show made up of The Searchers, Dusty Springfield, Manfred Mann and the Four Pennies. If it hadn't been for *Do Wah Diddy* and *Hard Days Night*, we could have reached Number 1, but we managed to sell 400,000 copies and become part of the Sixties pop scene, at last.

# *What Image?*

After four appearances on 'Top of the Pops' within a short space of time, we were well and truly established, but unaware of the importance of our 'Image'. Not enough careful thought went into the follow-up to the record and there was no one around to guide us. As we had not yet written another song, we recorded *Come To The Dance*, which was the opening track from the Four Preps album that Butch had bought for me the previous Christmas. We left the studio without a care in the world and we all felt, OK, what's next? With such a good song, we must have another hit, especially as we are now an established group . . . How wrong we were!

On the 28th August, we began a West Country tour, again with the Rolling Stones. Millie, the Overlanders and the Paramounts completed the line-up. (Gary Brooker, the Paramounts' keyboard player, eventually became the voice of Procol Harem and their guitarist Robin Trower became a huge success in the States.)

We began to benefit financially as our appearance fees increased, so I invested in a Hillman Imp. We gave the coach to the local Toc H and began to travel individually. Graham McCarther became our very first Road Manager and proved to be invaluable. I took the Imp on the Stones tour and invited Terry James, my old school pal, to come along. The compere on this tour was Gerry Clements, a Canadian who was completely out of his depth. He just couldn't handle the scream-ing fans and was therefore asked to go and join the Mounties! John Smith the tour promoter asked if *we* would introduce the Stones every night and as crowd reaction to Mick Jagger was much the same as Beatlemania, plenty of thought was needed as to how we would approach the task.

Butch and I took it in turns. I would go to the centre stage and as the kids knew who were behind the tabs, they were already going mad! I held up an old vest and said, 'Who does this belong to then, is it Millic's?' NO! ! ! !

'Then it must be Mick's.' YEA! ! ! ! . . . Screams . . . Chaos. I threw the vest into the crowd and shouted,

'The Rolling Stones', then I ran off the stage, jumped into the Imp with Terry and went back to the hotel for a beer! What else could I do? I had watched Rolf Harris suffer every

*Our wedding day, September 26, 1964.*

night at Finsbury Park and knew that anything more elaborate in the way of an introduction would have been wasted.

One thing was certain. The Stones knew exactly what *their* image was and they played up to it as much as they could.

The last night of the tour was at the Pavilion, Bournemouth, when Millie was replaced by Long John Baldry and the Hoochie Coochie Men, one of whom was a talented piano player called Reg Dwight, now Elton John.

We received great reviews in all the papers during this tour, but a particular word kept reappearing to describe us ... 'Novelty'. Perhaps our Image was exactly that and we hadn't had the intelligence to see it.

# *The Wedding*

The timing of the release of *Call Up The Groups* couldn't have been more perfect. Veronica and I had arranged our big day for the 26th September. Duke and his lady, Pauline, were to be married on the same day in Dunstable. The day started with a heavy downpour and knowing how nervous Veronica was, I sent a note to her, via my sister Margaret, to say that when the time came for her to walk down the aisle, the sun would shine through the stained glass windows; and it did too! I was feeling slightly the worse for wear myself as, needless to say, Duke and I had had a few jars the night before, after our show at the Streatham Ice Rink.

Perhaps because rumours had spread that Mick Jagger and the Stones were to be guests at our wedding, the church was completely surrounded by crowds, twenty people deep and although Veronica arrived on time, it was ten minutes before she was able to begin her walk up the aisle. Mr Claydon the organist played the tune to *You Were Made For Me* as she made her way towards me. Our wedding reception was held at the Hunt Hotel, next to the church, but because of the crowds, it took a long time to take all the photographs and we arrived an hour late! Unfortunately, the rest of the guests were blotto by then!

To the disappointment of the crowd, neither Mick nor any of the other Stones made an appearance that day. I hadn't invited them and I knew they wouldn't have come just for fun!

It was a great day and after a night at the Excelsior Hotel, Heathrow, we flew off to the Alps for two weeks' total peace and quiet.

## *Bertram Mills Circus*

*Come To The Dance* was released during the second week of October and only reached number 42. We were deeply upset that it didn't climb any higher, but it was a hard lesson we'd learned about how fickle the public can be. It was only after the event that we very quickly realised what image was all about. Hundreds of people said, 'Why didn't you release another comedy record?' We had been so wrapped up in our own little world in Leighton Buzzard that we didn't realise we had been 'pigeon-holed'. The Beatles and the Stones were Rock'n'Roll, Jim Reeves was Country and we were . . . Comedy, for ever.

Then, Tony pulled off another scoop! We ended 1964 at Bertram Mills Circus. For nine weeks we performed ten minutes per show at Olympia, their usual winter season venue. At first our relationship with the other acts was not too good, because they, quite rightly, wanted to keep the show traditional; but it didn't take too long to change all that. The elephant boys, the ring boys and the sons and daughters of the other acts were very happy to see a pop group in the middle of a ring, which proved not to be the easiest place to entertain, because we could only face one way. I always chuckle to myself when I hear that it takes two days to set the staging for a touring band, especially in today's world of modern technology. At the circus, the ring boys set our staging and amplification in under three minutes. They could dismantle it in even less time!

When Coco the Clown found out that my nickname was 'Peanuts', he introduced me to the 'Peanut Club', a charity organisation that raised money for the Burns Unit at East Grinstead Hospital. The Unit was founded by Sir Charles McIndoe during the Second World War and used mainly by the injured pilots.

I spent hours with Coco that winter. He used to tell me stories of his days in Russia and how he had planned his escape. His book was the first biography I'd ever read, so to hear the stories actually 'from the horse's mouth' was interesting to say the least.

The elephant boys were a tough lot. A small gang of trouble makers came to the side shows one day and began to shout abuse and generally cause trouble and a little fracas ensued. Needless to say, one of them ended up in hospital very badly beaten up. As he was due to be married the very next day, the boy responsible for his injuries felt that he should go to the hospital and apologise; which he did. However, after his little bedside speech, the patient said, 'When I get out of here, I'll come searching for you and you'll regret the day you were born.'

With that, elephant boy grabbed him from his bed and gave him another hiding that left him out cold for the house doctor's next visit!

# Palladium at Last

On the 21st February, 1965 we were back on tour, this time with Adam Faith and Sandie Shaw, who was the first woman I heard say the dreaded 'four letter' word. We were stepping off the tour bus, outside the Ipswich Gaumont on a very wet night indeed and she stepped straight into a puddle.

'Oh f . . . !' she said. Us country boys had never heard a lady swear like that before. Mr Faith kept himself separate from the rest of us. When we *did* see him, he was always doing crossword puzzles and I got the feeling he just wanted to get on and off stage as quickly as possible. His backing band were the Roulettes and included the prolific Russ Ballard.

We finished recording *Pop Go The Workers* on the 3rd March. This was our attempt to maintain our Image. Having put the groups into the Forces, we were now sending them out to do an honest days work! Our victims this time were the Supremes, the Batchelors, the Stones, the Beatles, Val Doonican and Sandie Shaw. The big hit line was a Butch special, 'I don't want to go to work, on me bike in the rain.' As the record reached no. 5 and stayed in the charts for 13 weeks, we realised that the public had formed their image of the Barron Knights and we would always be a novelty group. We had made a rod for our own backs and no matter how hard we tried, that would never change.

We were thrilled with our success and knowing that we had the comedy market to ourselves was a big morale-booster. Every TV show we appeared on wanted us to do a 'ditty' based on the news of the day; so we were like a travelling 'That Was The Week That Was'.

On the 28th March, 1965, after five years of being together in the band, we were asked to appear on 'Sunday Night at the London Palladium'. It was a fabulous feeling to think that at last we had made the top spot and I was about to stand on the very same stage where Slim Whitman had stood and go around the roundabout with the dancing girls! The night before the Palladium show, we had performed at the Wigan Casino and so by the time we arrived back in Leighton Buzzard, it was time to drive to London for the first rehearsal at 11 am. We were given about twenty minutes to complete the sound check and rehearse camera angles and it was daunting to stand on that empty stage in front of the empty theatre. Once the rehearsal was over, I took a walk along Carnaby Street and tried to take my mind off what was going to be the most important five minutes of my life. I found a cafe and seemed to be the only customer for lunch; after tasting it, I could understand why!

The show, which starred Eartha Kitt and was compered by Norman Vaughan, went like a dream and the Barron Knights' reputation grew stronger by the day.

It wasn't long before we were asked to do another show at the Palladium, but this time things didn't run so smoothly, although the result was to our advantage. During our Rolling Stones routine, I fell on my backside, smashing my guitar to the floor and the jack plug from the lead pierced the sound box causing the instrument to be very much out of tune. What I was supposed to do next, was to walk up to the microphone, play an arpeggio in B flat and in my Dudley Moore voice sing *Now Is The Time To Say Goodbye*. But on this occasion, every string was out of tune; I hit B flat and the audience went wild!

They laughed so much that I started giggling, then Butch became uncontrollable. I played another funny chord and eventually managed to sing, 'Now is the time to yield a sigh.' We were both out of control again and the crowd loved it. Having struggled through to the end of our short spot, we left the stage to cries of 'More!' A commercial break then followed and we walked off stage towards Jack Matthews, the stage manager. We could almost see the flames shooting out his ears, 'You will never work this theatre again. Over-running by two minutes is not allowed on a live television show. I never want to see you again.'

We were on such a high when we reached the dressing room, that we couldn't have given a hoot what Jack had said. We knew that the 18 million viewers saw us as a bunch of very entertaining, young guys who were placed in a situation that, handled the wrong way could have resulted in disaster. At the end of the show, we were on the roundabout and as our turn came to face the audience, the cheers rang louder. It was a memorable moment. It's strange that sometimes mishaps can lead to achievement!

Jack Matthews found out the next day that we were to do 26 weeks at the Palladium, with Ken Dodd, starting on the 17th April.

The fact that Ken Dodd had big record sales, combined with our own success, meant that the show was a winner from the very start. It broke all records and being a prestige show, it did us no harm at all; but we found it tough performing only 10 minutes a night for such a long season.

We appeared in more TV shows, including a couple more 'Top of the Pops' and the Jack Hylton Memorial Show, with Sophie Tucker, Marlene Deitrich, the Crazy Gang and what seemed like every other star who was alive at the time.

In mid-July, we managed a 'Blackpool Night Out' with Shirley Bassey, Billy Dainty and Mike and Bernie Winters. If there was a remote chance of doing a full show anywhere, we took it. Playing two Sunday concerts at the Bournemouth Pavilion was such a relief and we had a wonderful support act in an up-and-coming Welsh singer named Tom Jones. While old ladies walked out during his act, complaining that it was obscene, young ladies were wanting more of the hip-swaying Welshman.

On the 19th July that year, we set a record we've yet to break. At 11 am we performed at an outdoor concert in Bedford. We then had a Saturday matinee at the Palladium, plus the usual two evening shows, then when those were finished, it was off with the make-up and down to Midhurst in Sussex for Lord Cowdrey's son's 21st birthday celebrations. We slept well that night!

Butch decided to get married during the Palladium season and his Stag Night proved to be a colourful affair. After the show, having drunk enough to make the shares in Whitbreads rise, he ended up on the dressing room floor unable to move, while the dancing girls ripped off his clothes and smothered him in lipstick. We then carried him to Graham's car and, like a good roadie should, he drove him home and put him to bed. We arrived at the church in Hemel Hempstead at 11 am next morning, to find a very ill-looking Butch. His wife, Chris, looked wonderful in her beautiful white dress, the colour of which matched Butch's face perfectly. We gave him a week off for his honeymoon and trained Dev Douglas so that he could stand in while Butch was away. Not only was he the same size for the suit, but he was very similar to Butch in looks.

Because of the phenomenal success of the Palladium show, we were all asked to extend the season. This was not an arrangement we could be happy about, because we'd had other work offered to us where we could earn much more money and be able to perform our full show, instead of the 10 minutes

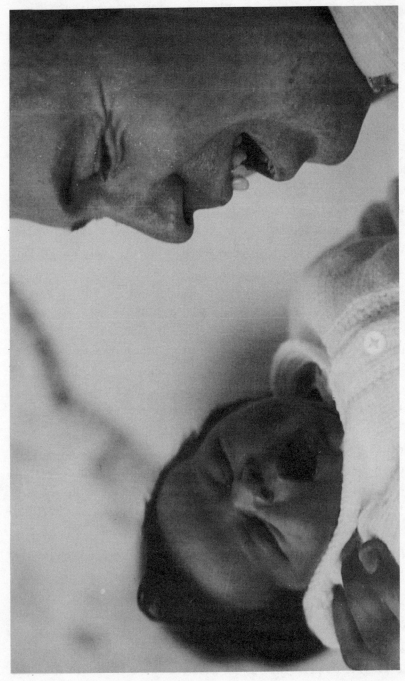

*With my daughter, Tanya, 2 days old. September 1965. The first Barron Knight Baby.*

we were doing at present. Tony went to discuss the situation with the Bernard Delfont Organisation, who tried to persuade us to agree by telling him that the whole show had been booked for the Royal Command Performance and they would take us off if we didn't agree to extend our contract. This upset Tony, very much; we had served them well by giving them a super show for 26 weeks at half our normal fee. Because both Doddy and we were probably, at that time, the biggest draws in the country, they were taking fortunes every week in ticket sales and it would be so easy for them to book another act, but very difficult for us to cancel lots of bookings. They wouldn't agree to raise our fee, so Tony pulled us off the show on the 11th September.

The following month, the whole show appeared on the Royal Command Performance . . . except for us!

It was sad to leave such a happy show in that way. I did, however, make a good friend of Jack Matthews, who was sometimes misunderstood but always most professional at his job.

On Sunday, 26th September, 1965 all thoughts of the Barron Knights were forgotten when Veronica presented me with an 8lb 4oz baby daughter, Tanya.

# Panto

1965 had been a great year for us. Having had one hit record in March, it looked highly likely that we would end the year with our first Christmas release, *Merry Gentle Pops*. The victims this time were Donovan, Marianne Faithfull, the Hollies, Ivy League, Pete and Dud and the omnipresent Rolling Stones. Our first live performance of this track took place at the Wembley Arena during the 'Glad Rag Ball' which had quite a big bill and included The Who, Georgie Fame, Donovan, the Hollies, the Merseybeats, The Byrds, Wilson Pickett, and the Ram Jam Band. Although they all set up massive sound systems, you couldn't hear a word that anyone was singing: but we set up our tiny little speakers and 7000 people heard every word.

Our first panto was at the Alexander Theatre, Birmingham. We were entering into a very different area of show business and thus meeting people who were strict professionals. Robinson Crusoe here we come!

Derek Salberg, the theatre owner, was also the producer and insisted on two weeks' rehearsal. Ruth Madoc was the leading lady and Denny Willis, the comedian. He had the funniest comedy routine that we had ever seen. Called 'The Quorn', it consisted of four men who stood in line, looking very smart in their red hunting attire, singing about chasing the fox. At the same time, they made movements appertaining to the words, with Denny at one end trying to get the actions correct. It was slapstick at its best and never failed to create huge gales of laughter from the audience. We played the jolly sailors that had been shipwrecked and kept popping on and off to sing various songs.

It was ironic that we were then in competition with Doddy, who was at the other big theatre in town. However, *Merry Gentle Pops* was at No. 9 in the charts so *our* business was most satisfactory. After our Christmas Eve opening, Mr Salberg hosted a little party to say thank you and he ended his brief speech by saying, 'I think we will have a successful season, Dodd willing.'

We tried very hard to enter into the spirit of panto and I'm sure it was all part of the learning process, but after our fifth one in 1969, we called it a day.

★

68

*Now you know why we won't do panto again.*

*Great Yarmouth, 1966. L. to R. Myself, Donald Peers, Ted Rogers, Teddy Johnson and Butch.*

*Adam Faith tour, 1966. Top, L. to R. Butch, Dave, Phil Wainman, Robin Trower, Patrick Kerr. Bottom, L. to R. Duke, Barron, Gary Brooker.*

71

A pattern of work began to emerge with Summer Season and Panto being the bases from which we worked. In between, there were 'one niters' and the odd cabaret club. It all looked very rosy for us with lots of work, money and fun. But one of the problems becoming obvious to us was that all the Panto/ Summer Season work was only allowing us the maximum of thirty minutes to perform our act, so it became increasingly difficult to develop and experiment. When we did go back on the road, we always felt as though we were starting all over again.

Our first summer season was in 1966, at Great Yarmouth ABC Theatre with Ted Rodgers and Frank Ifield (not forgetting Tanya the elephant). Frank Ifield was such a big hit in the mid-Sixties, that consequently every night at the ABC was a sell-out. He sang so well and could still be a big star today had he not changed his style to country music. From a career point of view it was not the best of moves as his popularity suffered once he was away from the public eye. If it was his choice because of his love for country music, then so be it. We still see Frank once a year when we tour Australia and although a lung complaint has prevented him from performing for many years, he still gets involved with young talent, helping them along the path to success that he once walked.

Two cups were won during that Yarmouth season. England won the World Cup and the Dickie Henderson Golf Trophy went to yours truly!

The golf bug bit me in 1964, and like all potential Arnold Palmers, I wanted to beat the world as soon as possible, so all my spare hours and more were spent hitting golf balls on the practice ground.

Gorleston Golf Club is about four miles outside Great Yarmouth and I think I must have covered about every square inch of that course. Visiting artistes were always treated as if they were members and I played five days a week for ten weeks at a cost of about £10.

Dickie Henderson was a great practical joker and one morning at Gorleston, I was playing with Ted Rodgers while up ahead Dickie was playing with Albie Keen. They disappeared over the hill, so I drove off. We walked up to the top of the hill to find Albie bending over a prostrate Mr Henderson and giving every indication that he was trying to revive him. I quickened my pace and began to worry that I had hit him with my golf ball.

'I should have waited longer; he won't be able to do the show tonight.' All these dreadful thoughts were going through my head. I reached the body and anxiously looked down. Dickie opened one eye and said, 'Mine's a gin and tonic.'

My ball had actually reached them, so they decided to teach me a lesson as I hadn't waited for the bell to be rung to signify that it was all clear!

A french horn player who was in the pit orchestra, was extremely keen on the game but was one of those people who would never play golf to a high standard, no matter how hard he tried. On one occasion, he was so frustrated with his game, he decided to give it all up in great style. He hit three consecutive balls into the pond on the right of the eighth tee and with his last ball said, 'If this goes in the pond, so will the clubs'.

It did and with that he picked up his bag and trolley and threw the lot into the water. He then took the shortest route to the bar and slowly drowned his sorrows while telling us all that he would never touch another golf club as long as he lived. After about an hour he got up and walked in the direction of the pond. We thought, 'Hello, he's changed his mind quickly.' He took his shoes and socks off, rolled up his trousers and waded in to the pond to retrieve his clubs . . . or so we thought. Dragging the clubs out of the water, he unzipped the side pocket, took out his car keys, then lifted the bag above his head and threw them back in the water. Everyone in the bar joined together in a huge round of applause!

# Straight Records

Once the summer season was over, EMI were harassing us again to write another comedy medley. We were still very inexperienced when it came to Image and Marketing and no one could convince us that we couldn't be successful in releasing a serious record. During a two year period, we'd had three big hits with the subjects of the Forces, Work and Christmas. We thought that the idea must be wearing thin but EMI didn't agree. So, taking their advice, we put our heads together and produced *Under New Management*, a story about the groups being in Parliament. This time we used the Troggs, Dave Berry, David and Jonathan, Lovin' Spoonful, the Beach Boys and the Bonaparte novelty song *They're Coming To Take Me Away*. In case the DJ's were thinking, as we were, that the idea was stale, we made a big effort to keep a very high standard of humour, which resulted in the song reaching number 15 in the charts. We were pleased to admit that EMI had been right.

It was getting impossible to maintain such a standard of humour on record. Writing a comedy sketch is easy compared to writing lyrics that still have to be funny even after the twentieth time of listening. We were very good at it, but thought that the whole idea should be 'put on ice' and allowed to be forgotten until a new generation were ready to be entertained. We had reached the stage where we thought we could record a serious song that, if good enough, the public would go out and buy. After all, fans were constantly saying how good our vocal sound was and why didn't we record an appropriate song to show it off.

Although I was heavily involved with writing comedy, I hadn't stopped pursuing the idea of creating love songs.

*Promotion for Under New Management.*

75

Everything I wrote, I played to Cyril Shane, at that time a very successful Jewish publisher. He sat me down one day and told me that my writing was 'Out of town', and to go home and start again. This I did and my first attempt with the new approach was *Come On In*. I couldn't believe how much he liked it. Within weeks he 'phoned to tell me that it had been recorded by Richard Antony, the successful French artiste. I was more than pleased, as it was the first time that one of my songs had been recorded by someone else. I then told Cyril that the Barron Knights' intentions were to record a serious song and he sorted out a few demo's for me to take back to Leighton Buzzard. Most of them were American songs and included in the pile was *He Aint Heavy, He's My Brother!* It was not the best of demo's, but that was no excuse for not spotting what would be a massive hit. In the course of many weeks spent visiting all the publishers, another song I selected was *Here Comes The Night*, but again, the boys were not too keen! We ended up by recording a Pete Townsend song, *Lazy Fat People*. It was a good attempt, but the BBC thought otherwise!

A flower-power song was next, *Here Come The Bees*, then a slushy ballad, *I Never Will Marry*. The results were dreadful. It seemed that no radio station around would play anything serious by the Barron Knights and thus we were getting more and more despondent about our recording career, although thankfully, the live work was earning us lots of money.

1968 was Olympic year and although it didn't comply with our future ambitions, we decided to write another medley about the pop stars becoming athletes. We used the Small Faces, Des O'Connor, Tom Jones, Esther and Abi Ofarim and Mama Cass. Although it wasn't our best effort, EMI did not help the situation at all when you consider that the Olympics were held in the summer and they decided not to release the song until October. It was a bad move and cost us thousands of record sales. However, it did reach number 35!

In 1969, EMI had decided that if we were to have a straight hit, then we needed a good producer to sort it all out. Up to that point we had had total control over what we released, but by this time we felt we had lost our way. In-house producer, Wally Ridley, took us under his wing and at the first meeting in his office overlooking Manchester Square, he played us several exellent songs. He decided on *Love And The World Loves With You*, an Alan Hawkshaw composition, arranged and conducted by Richard Holmes. It was a pleasant little song and nothing more, and the number of times it was played on the radio matched the number of sales . . . Nowt!

Wally then pulled a much better song out of his bag! *Traces* was a beautiful melodic, mid-tempo, love song. We made a good job of the track and it sounded similar to the Four Seasons' hit version of *I've Got You Under My Skin*. Once again, much to everybody's disappointment, the public didn't hear it because it wasn't played on the radio. The only consolation was that *we* were very proud of it.

Shortly after the release of *Traces*, the inevitable happened and EMI refused to renew our contract. We had plenty to thank them for. They were instrumental in making us a household name and because of that we could work and make a very good living for the rest of our lives.

# *Blackpool*

We are constantly being asked the same question, which is, 'Where do you like working the most?'

It's difficult to answer that because there are so many places where we enjoy performing. An easier question to answer would be, 'Where do you least like working?' For me, the answer to that would be Blackpool. There, we have the largest summer resort in the country, with as many shows as Las Vegas, but for some strange reason our act never gets the reaction it deserves. We perform in all the Northern towns and the resulting laughter will be the same as down South, but put the same audience in a Blackpool theatre and we wonder what we've done wrong!

Our first Blackpool season was in 1967, again with Frank Ifield. The comedian was Jimmy Tarbuck and every night he would go on stage, do all the old standard seaside gags and get belly laughs. We would do our twenty-minute spot full of funny, topical lines and all we would get would be titters! I used to visit other shows to see what reaction other acts were experiencing; I discovered that Bruce Forsyth and Millicent Martin were having the same trouble. They were using such good material and working so hard, but for nothing. The Blackpool audience just didn't understand what they or we were doing. Jimmy Tarbuck was a regular opponent of mine on the golf course and during a game I told him about the problems we were experiencing and he said, 'Only do jokes that they're familiar with; it means they haven't got to think. Remember they are on holiday and are here to relax, not to be educated.'

A few years later, we topped the bill at the North Pier and we still refused to change the show just for Blackpool. Consequently, we were very unhappy with the results. It really affected Barron. He began to hate the thought of stepping on stage and became so uptight that with about three weeks of a ten week season still to go, he had a nervous breakdown and ended up in hospital.

Since 1972, we have hardly worked in the town, not even a Sunday concert. However, in 1990 we provided the show for the Blackpool Landladies at one of the town's big hotels and much to our surprise they gave us a fantastic reception. Blackpool will always remain one of life's mysteries.

## Stoned Again

We managed one more tour with the Rolling Stones; this time with Peter & Gordon and compere, the mad Tony Marsh. Two of the funniest moments occurred on this tour. Peter & Gordon were totally opposite to the rest of us on the show. Gordon Waller was like a hyper-active squirrel, while Peter Asher sat quietly in a corner and chewed on his nails. They both spoke extremely well, but were so nervous, they couldn't even give the appearance of being confident on stage.

The theatre in Cannock seemed just about ready for the demolition boys. It had one long, narrow dressing-room with plaster falling off the wall, which was not the best place to spend a few hours while waiting for the show to start. As usual, the whole place was surrounded with Stones' fans screaming for Mick or Brian. On this particular night, Peter Asher had his girlfriend, the original Sloane Ranger, in tow, and made the dressing-room seem even more crowded. Suddenly, there was an awful smell; there was no noise, but it was obvious that someone had broken wind. Mick turned to Brian and said, 'Was that you?' Brian replied, 'No, it was her,' pointing at Peter's girlfriend. Mick giggled and said, 'That's what you call a society fart.'

As the dressing room erupted, the poor girl went scarlet!

Peter didn't say a word. That 'poor girl' was Chrissie Shrimpton, sister of famous model Jean.

Peter now lives in Los Angeles managing James Taylor and Linda Ronstadt and I've no doubt that he and Mick have met many times since that day in Cannock, with no mention of the 'society fart'.

Incident number two happened at the Slough Adelphi. Tony Marsh, the compère, always did enjoy a few drinks and while the Stones were on stage whipping up a storm, he must, on this occasion, have experienced the same excitement as the young teenage girls in the front row. He went to the wings, dropped his trousers and shook his backside to the crowd. A few weeks later, in the County Court, he was fined £200 for indecent exposure. The following day, the newspaper read as follows: 'Mr Tony Marsh, the compère on the recent Rolling Stones tour, did indecently show his buttocks to the audience, while the Stones were singing *Make Love To Me*.' Tony was a laugh a minute, but after that tour, he was never seen or heard of again.

Barron had an unfortunate short conversation with Brian Jones on the last night of the tour. He said, 'My mother said to me today, "Are you still with those awful Rolling Stones?"'

Brian snapped back, 'F...! your mother.' Barron, forever the gentleman, just smiled politely and walked away.

Charlie hardly ever said a word and when he did it was usually to ask our drummer Dave to tune his kit. They were a good bunch of blokes and in the short time that we spent with them during their historic career, we had quite a few laughs together.

It seems strange that the two most popular groups ever to grace a slice of vinyl lost their founder members and thinkers of the band. Without doubt, John Lennon and Brian Jones held those positions.

# Leighton Buzzard

When we were kids, Leighton Buzzard was a sleepy little market town, where it was usual to see bicycles propped up against walls and pavements. Tuesday was market day, when the high street was full of farm animals in their pens, pubs were open all day and a cafe closed for lunch! On Sundays, families could be seen walking along the canal bank, dodging the fishermen's tackle; young boys would spend the day train spotting, with a bottle of Tizer to keep them company.

Progress has come to stand in the way of many of those happy moments. Like so many towns now, we have roads that are difficult to cross, one way streets, double the population and half the conversation, because people are too busy to have time to speak.

The shopkeepers were a wonderful bunch; so full of character and charm. Sadly they are now but few. Buildings of great beauty have been demolished and replaced by modern supermarkets and chain stores. If only there were more Eric Linneys around!

Eric was a small, white-haired man with a healthy complexion and a strong determination that his shop should remain untouched. His was a saddlery business and sports shop which was housed in a unique building of architectural interest. Although it was terraced, his place caught the eye, with its signs, wood and windows, so full of character. Inside the shop, the smell of leather and linseed oil greeted you as you walked on well-worn, polished floorboards. The business had been established for over sixty years, when along came a developer who wanted to buy up the whole site, knock it down and replace it with something that could have been designed by a four-year-old child.

'On your bike!', said Mr Linney, and that was his final word.

All the retail shops around him gave in, but dear old Eric became the thorn in the side of the developers and no way was he going to buckle to any offer. For weeks and months they tried everything, but no sweetener was going to work. The result was that Linney's shop is now flanked by boring new shops that highlight the beauty of the old.

Eric still maintains the 'closed for lunch' system, which gave rise to a story that has graced many a dinner party, in all four corners of the world. Butch had a very good neighbour, Ian the policeman, who wanted a new tracksuit, so off he went to the one and only sports shop around, Linney's. Eric 'junior' served him at around about 12.50 pm. Having found out his size, Eric handed three tracksuits of different colours to Ian and asked him to go into the cubicle to try them on. After about ten minutes, having decided on the colour, Ian drew back the curtain to find a darkened shop interior. He called for Eric, but Eric had gone . . . to lunch! Ian tried the shop door; it was locked! Being a policeman with a logical brain, he went into the office at the back of the shop and found Eric's home number.

'Hello, is that you, Eric?'

'Yes,' said Eric, 'who's that?'

'Ian,' said Ian.

'What do you want? I'm having my lunch,' replied Eric. That was when Ian said those magic words, 'I'll have the blue one.' He put down the phone and waited for Eric to return from lunch.

Thank God for those characters, of which Leighton Buzzard had its fair share.

Until recently, Griffin Brothers was the main electrical shop in the town, with a commanding position on the sunny side of the high street. The goods were sparsely displayed, much of the stock being 'out the back'. Len was always there behind the counter, with a fag in his mouth and on most occasions, whatever item you required was 'out the back'. He would greet you with the words, 'Hello Pete, how's your mum?' If Butch went in there, again it was 'How's your mum?' It became a catch phrase.

Shortly after Christmas, about ten years ago, we were taking down the decorations at home when Veronica noticed a bulb from the tree lights had blown. Off to Griffins she went with the faulty lights.

'Hello Len.'

'Hello Veronica, how's your mum?'

She explained about the lights, left them, and off she went to do more shopping. Eleven months later, I went up into the loft to fetch the Christmas decorations. Veronica noticed that the tree lights were missing and it took her quite a few minutes to realise what she had done the previous January. Down to Griffins she went.

'Hello Len.'

'Hello Veronica , how's your mum?'

'Do you remember, last January, I gave you some Christmas tree lights to fix?' Len said, 'Hang on love, let me go out the back.' Five minutes later he came back blowing dust off a box.

'Are these the ones?' he asked.

'Yes they are,' replied Veronica.

Len looked very sheepish and said, 'They'll be ready Thursday.'

Our little town had some amazing shopkeepers, considering that some had disabilities. Joe worked in Andersons, the photographers. He only had one arm, but with a thumb-nail like a Stanley knife, he could cope with anything you asked. With this human tool, he would open a camera, rip open the box that contained the film and put the film in the camera so that it was ready for use. He could fit a 13 amp plug in half the time that it takes me, all because of this 'Stanley knife'.

83

Brantoms, the pet food shop, employed a dear old chap who suffered with a bad shake. If you asked for a pound of bird seed, he would go to a big brown bag with his brass scoop and try to transfer the amount required onto the scales. It was quite a messy affair!

Ron Sewell the tailor was extremely short sighted. If I walked into the shop he would say, 'Hello ... ', then walk to within about two inches of my face and say 'Pete'.

To measure anyone for a suit must have been a nightmare for him. He would hold the tape measure to your arm, bring it up to his eyes to read the number and then bend down close to his book to write in the measurements. However, one thing was certain, the suit would be a beautiful fit and you could pay for it at a pound a week!

The Avery brothers owned the local garage and the last survivor of the trio is Brian. To this day he will check your tyres by kicking them. His disability is a bruised toe! If we broke down two hundred miles from home at 2 am on a foggy winter's night, Brian would be there to help us out. We treasure Brian and all the folks in Leighton Buzzard. We've needed them and still do.

## Australia '70

Apart from Tito's Club, Majorca in 1969 and of course the Hamburg fortnight, we hadn't been overseas to show the people in other countries the little talents we possessed.

On Good Friday, March 1970, we boarded the Pan Am 707

*Saying 'Tatty Bye' to Ken Dodd after 26 weeks at the London Palladium.*

*Ooooh! Betty.*

*Deep concentration at the Conservative Club, Bedford, 1961.*

*The first ever picture of the Barron Knights,
1960. Top, Dave Morrow and Don Ringsell.
Side, Juj Hopkins and Pete Langford.
Bottom, Tony Osmond.*

*As we are today, April 1993. John Shearer,
left, Garth Watt-Roy, far right.*

*The cast of the Beatles Christmas Show, 1963. John, Paul, Ringo,*
*George, Cilla Black, Rolf Harris, Fourmost, Billy J. Kramer,*
*Tommy Quickly and ourselves.*

*Winners of the Club Entertainers of the Year, 1977. Presented by*
*David Jacobs. Vince Hill is behind Barron and to the right are Dana and*
*Tom O'Connor.*

*End of show party, Durban, 1974. Petula Clarke, top left.*
*Bottom, L. to R. Lennie and Margaret Bennett, Duke, Tony and yours truly.*

*'Who Cut Your Hair'? Meeting my favourite royal, H.R.H. Princess Anne.*
*Billy Marsh is in the centre.*

*Our first mode of transport. Note Barron's spelling. He thought there were two R's in Baron and that's the way it stayed.*

*Our home for two years. And very comfy too.*

*What will the BBC think of next? 1970.*

*With Beach Boys, Mike Love, Al Jardine, Brian Wilson. Cardiff, 1974.*

*Ready Steady Go, 1964.*

*Bournemouth, 1961. L. to R. Dave Morrow, Juj Hopkins, Dickie Demon,*
*Barron Antony, myself and Don Ringsell.*

*The Show Biz Eleven, Blackpool, 1967. Jimmy Tarbuck and Bruce Forsyth are in the back row, Dickie Henderson and Andy Stewart in the front.*

*The winners of the British Rock and Pop Awards. L. to R. Dave, Gerry Rafferty, Butch, Robin Gibb, Bev Bevan (ELO), Ian Dury, Jeff Lynne, Me, Barron, Nick Lowe, Leo Sayer and Duke.*

bus-stop flight to Australia. It was called the bus-stop jet, because it stopped more times than the London bus from Ealing to Barkingside. It seemed that if the pilot looked down and saw a row of lights, he would land, pick up a fare and take off again. Our route from London was via Paris, Rome, Istanbul, Beirut, Karachi, Calcutta, Rangoon, Hong Kong, Jakarta and finally Sydney. I sent postcards to Veronica and all my friends to show where I'd been, but really all we saw of any of those places was the inside of the air terminal. We had to change aircraft at Hong Kong, which involved a two-hour wait, so we found the nearest toilet, had a good wash and brush-up and then found a comfortable seat on which to sit and write the postcard. The seats were back-to-back benches and as soon as I sat down I heard voices that I recognised coming from behind me. It was Hope and Keen, the comedy double act with whom we had spent two summer seasons. They were also on their way to Australia, but had stopped off in Hong Kong in order to have suits made.

Calcutta wasn't the most friendly place we visited! For some reason the aircraft had to park on a small runway at some distance from the terminal, but we were allowed out for fresh air, if that's what you could call it; it was like being in an oven with the smell of a blocked sewer. A little man came riding by on his 1935 black ladies bicycle, with his off-white turban plonked on his head and his Gandhi robe tucked up under his bum to avoid the spoke wheels. He looked such a friendly chap until he gave a throaty grunt and spat at us. I wouldn't have minded, but we hadn't sung a note! He's probably living in Bradford now, above the Himalaya Tandoori restaurant. I just hope he's kicked the spitting habit!

We landed in Sydney at about 8 am, 36 hours after leaving London. What happened next made me feel quite dirty. Having been told to remain in our seats, an Aussie, in his shorts, walked

*Sydney, Australia, 1970. The opera house was still under construction.*

through the middle aisle, spraying the cabin. (I felt like lifting my arms up and asking him for a quick squirt.) Apparently, it was done to kill any germs that may have been floating around; nevertheless, we found it all very strange. The customs officer searched my case, took away my golf shoes and dipped them into another germ-killing substance. God knows what they would do to the Rolling Stones, who were due to arrive there the following day.

Our agent in Australia was Jim Mcdonald. His office was in a block of flats that he owned at South Avenue, Double Bay, (nicknamed 'Double Pay' because of its expensive shops) and the five of us, plus Tony Avern, were to share one of the flats. We dumped our cases and immediately went our separate ways; some to the pub, others to their bed but I went to Bondi beach to get sunburned. The Aussie accent is not the most attractive in the world, but within hours of treading on that red soil, we were all slipping into the famous drawl as quickly as we were making friends. The pub regulars thought we were 'good blokes' and not bad for Poms; but we found out that most of the crinkly skinned locals were actually from the Mother Country and wanted to know if West Street in Gravesend had changed!

Sydney is unique for having what they call League Clubs. These are entertainment centres that provide facilities for tennis, bowls, restaurants and cabaret. The large ones also have a premier rugby football team that enjoys popularity similar to that of Spurs or Arsenal. The biggest is St Georges League Club and that was where we made our Australian debut and began a four-week season.

I couldn't believe how many big American stars had been there and as we were following the Sammy Davis Jnr Show, we had to be on our toes! It was a Las Vegas style production which consisted of a fourteen piece orchestra, eight dancing girls, a compere/singer/comedian and then the lads from

Leighton Buzzard. We had a wonderful time. The audience was full of British immigrants who made us feel at home, while we reminded them of the same.

At a party given by Jim Mcdonald, I met Wayne Yates, who was to become a long-standing family friend. He was very smartly dressed, well-mannered and not at all like the image of the typical Australian male. He didn't have a beer belly and would never be heard to shout or swear in front of women, but he did have a wonderful sense of humour, albeit slightly warped! One Sunday morning he took me to Tamarama beach just south of Bondi. The surf was high and it was a scorcher of a day but Wayne wasn't interested in acquiring a tan, just in the height of the waves. We were watching the swimmers who were body-surfing about a hundred yards out when he asked if I'd like to try. He handed me a flipper and instead of swimming out from the beach we walked along the rocks and dived in where the waves were breaking.

Having caught a couple of small waves just to get the feel of things, I was now ready for the big one, or so I thought! About a dozen of us were treading water, waiting, when all of a sudden, it was on its way. We all found our 'go for it' positions and away we went, hoping to ride this monster. I caught it brilliantly and felt as though I was flying in the wind; I could feel the water vibrating on my stomach as I was lifted about eight feet in the air. In a flash the wave broke and I was flung towards the sea bed. I hit the sand hard and twisted and turned until I finally managed to surface.

That was enough! I didn't want any more of that, so I went back to the beach for a quiet sunbathe. I lay there, motionless, for an hour before deciding that it was time to get back for a shower before the show. It was then that I discovered that I couldn't move. There was the most awful pain at the base of my spine and I knew that I had inflicted serious damage on my back. I could hardly get myself into Wayne's car, but thought

88

that a hot bath would ease the pain . . . No chance! As show time crept nearer, my back got worse and I found that I had to limp and stoop to be comfortable. That show was a blur and I was relieved to lie flat on the dressing-room floor, whenever possible.

Wayne had very kindly offered to take me out for a late meal in Double Bay and had chosen the restaurant very carefully. It was Turkish and situated above a shoe shop, but climbing the flight of stairs that night was like conquering the Eiger! During the meal, we sat on very large cushions, which Wayne had thought would be helpful for the pain I was suffering. I tried to drink the pain away and after lots of fun and jollification, we paid the bill and prepared to leave, but . . . I was stuck. I couldn't get off the cushion without help, so Wayne hoisted me up and helped me to walk out. As we were walking down the stairs, a couple of people were coming up and as I couldn't stand up straight, they gave me a good stare. I stopped them in their tracks, put my hand on the painful spot and said, 'Don't have the soup.'

When they were out of sight, Wayne hit the floor and became uncontrollable with laughter. We laughed until my insides ached. I've seen him every year since and we never fail to remind ourselves of that very painful night. Even if he writes a letter, the PS is always 'Don't have the soup!'

I've spent a fortune trying to fix my back; but as back sufferers well know, the pain always returns when you least expect it.

I wasn't the only one in the band to have trouble with the South Pacific. Barron and Dave were put off sea water for life. While they were spending a quiet afternoon on Coogee beach, they decided to have a dip to cool off, but were unaware of the 'Rip', an under-current that can whip your legs away and carry you thirty yards out to sea within seconds. They were both doing the pommy crawl when they were dragged out to the

North end of the bay, only to be buffeted against the jagged rocks, causing them to be covered in hundreds of little razor cuts. Out came the big beefy Lifeguards with their ropes and told the pair they'd better swim between the flags next time.

The Aussies certainly like to live the outdoor life and we wanted to sample every aspect. Their beautiful weather tempts you to stay with the water sports. Barron was a very keen water skier and I too had sampled the thrill of being towed behind a boat at breakneck speed, so off we went to the Hawkesbury River, about an hour's journey North of the city.

We had survived a few runs up and down and were enjoying every moment. What happened next could only be seen in a cartoon of Roadrunner! I was out of the wake and enjoying the scenery when a tree appeared in front of me, floating across my path. Before I could think, the tips of my skis hit the tree, I was catapulted into the air and then crashed into the water. The driver turned the boat around to pick up me and my skis and was convinced that I had broken my legs, but by a miracle I was all in one piece. I certainly didn't want to carry on then, so he dropped me off and as I jumped off the boat I trod on something very sharp and gashed the bottom of my foot. It was quite a deep and nasty cut that took a while to heal, so my water sports were over for a few days.

The next adventure was painful to watch. Butch, Tony and I decided that we wanted to see a Kangaroo. The nearest place was Ku-ring-gai Chase, a National Park, again north of Sydney and about an hour's drive away. We hired a car and over the bridge we went, in order to find these wonderful creatures in their natural habitat. Walking through the rugged bushland, we felt that this was the Australia we had seen in school books and it wasn't long before we would have done anything for a couple of cans of Fosters, but there were no pubs out there, just the odd stem of dry grass. We eventually reached the area where the kangaroos were and they were obviously used to human beings as they showed no fear at all. Butch had half a packet of crisps in his pocket, so he thought he'd give them a little treat. Out came my camera to record it all for the folks back home.

'Here Joey Joey,' Butch whispered.

A couple of kangaroos hopped towards him and had a nibble of what was on offer. They weren't too keen on the taste, and they showed it! One Joey sat back on his tail and gave Butch a kick right in the area that makes men exclaim more than 'Oh dear'. Poor Butch was doubled up in pain as Tony and I had a chuckle to each other. I recorded the incident on film and to this day Butch has yet to see the result of my timing. Maybe the heat had affected me that day, but within minutes of us laughing at Butch, I fed the Kangaroos with peppermints and was kicked in exactly the same spot . . . You have to be tough to survive in the bush!

As if I hadn't had my share of mishaps, two days later I was a front seat passenger being driven over the harbour bridge, during a heavy downpour, when the car in front performed a wonderful 180 degree turn and we hit it full on. Now my shoulder hurt as well as my back and Duke had gashed his nose rather badly.

Sunday, 10th April, 1970 was my 27th birthday and we were still at St Georges League Club. Sunday shows always took place in the late afternoon and finished about 7 pm. After the show on this particular night, I went into the audience to talk to a table of English folks. I had been there quite a time and was just beginning to worry that the boys might be waiting for me, when Tony joined the table and assured me that there was no problem as they had already gone and he and I would go back to Double Bay in the second car at our leisure. We'd all been talking away for ages when I suddenly realised that it was 9 pm and I was starving; so I nudged Tony and off we went back to the flat. It was in complete darkness, so I fumbled for the key

*Seconds later I was on my knees. Kuringi Chase. North Sydney, 1971.*

92

and as I opened the door I remember saying, 'Bloody hell Tony, I could murder a f . . . . . g pizza.'

To my surprise, the lights came on and a room full of tanned people sang *Happy Birthday* to me. The boys and Wayne had arranged the whole thing and to this day I can't remember the last drink. It certainly numbed all my aches and pains!

On this particular trip, Sydney was really all we saw of Australia, but we loved every moment. We had many more trips when we managed to cover the whole country and had more 'hairy' moments that I will share with you, later.

# *The Seventies*

It was the beginning of a new decade and I wondered if the end of the Barron Knights was in sight. There was an air of contentment in the band because of all the live work that was available, but the constant touring would surely take its toll. I would have been happier if we had had a recording contract, because being 'in the charts' was so important to me, but the feeling amongst the rest of the boys was, 'no more funny records'. It was always a thrill for me when we were recording at Lansdowne and then at Abbey Road Studios. There were so many good moments. When we were in the middle of recording *An Olympic Record*, who should walk into the studio, but Paul McCartney! Abbey Road had then been their home for about three weeks. He said, 'Hi fellas, would you like to here our new single?'

He sat down at the big, black, grand piano, fiddled with a few chords, and after a slight pause he began to sing, 'Hey Jude, don't make it bad . . .' Halfway through he forgot the words, but soon recovered to complete the song and then asked what we thought. It was such a wonderful moment we were almost speechless. Can you imagine us bursting in on a Beatles session while they were recording *Strawberry Fields Forever* and singing to them our new lyrics to a Des O'Connor song?

Back in that summer of '68 we were driving down to Brighton with the radio blasting away and we heard, 'And here it is, straight in at number one *Hey Jude* by the Beatles.' It sounded so good, it made me shiver.

Were the Seventies going to provide such memories? I doubted it very much, knowing the direction in which we seemed to be going. With a summer season at Skegness with Donald Peers and at Brighton the following year with Dick Emery, we were certainly cashing in on our success, but not investing in the future to provide us with 'continued success'.

At the end of Skegness pier was a theatre that had provided twenty years of Old Time Music Hall. When the local council decided it was time for a change and asked us if we would be prepared to bring in a modern summer show, we were pleased to accept both the challenge and the excellent fees they offered. We filled the theatre every night for eight weeks and Skegness became a venue of major consideration for many stars.

We all had a great time in 'Skeggie'. My golf was steadily improving with the help of Ron Squires, the North Shore Golf Club professional, and Duke, without the aid of a map, found all the hotel bars without once getting lost! Barron became so proficient at water skiing, he bought his own power boat, of which he was so proud until the day it nearly killed his lovely wife, Val! They were on the lake having a quiet ski when Barron decided he wanted to have a go at the jump. Val was in the driving seat and began to increase the speed as she headed for the big sloping wooden platform and began to turn away from it slightly. As soon as she realised that the steering wheel wasn't doing what she wanted it to, she tried to turn away from the platform, but it was too late! The front of the boat hit the jump and twisted sideways; the engine went the other way, which automatically brought the boat to a standstill.

A very frightened Val looked around for Barron, who had seen what was happening and let go of the tow rope before swimming towards the boat. Thank God all was well, except that they were minus one Volvo engine. Their friend 'Dobbo' had seen everything from his boat, so within seconds he was on the scene, and with the help of a pair of goggles, eventually recovered the engine. The three of them then called it a day and ended up in the best fish and chip cafe in town called ... 'Dobbo's'.

There are two golf courses in Skegness, North Shore and Seacroft. Being a member of the Vaudeville Golfing Society entitled me to membership for the season at North Shore where I played with Ron Squires twice a week. If he sank a long putt he would always say 'I dyked it'. He had the most interesting East Lincolnshire accent! Twenty years later I was in Skegness in search of Ron, only to find that he had gone to that fairway in the sky.

Seacroft was, and still is, a tough test for any good golfer. My handicap was eight during that period, but with the sea breeze to contend with, I needed all my skill to play to it. Donald Peers wouldn't play North Shore, only Seacroft and it was easy to understand why. The first tee was equal to many greens and the rest of the course was beautifully manicured.

Donald was a great player and a wonderful teacher. He studied the game and made it his job to understand the swing that we all seem to make appear so difficult. We would usually play eighteen holes, have a pot of tea and a sandwich, then go back to the practice ground for a chipping competition. He taught me the art of keeping the game simple and what he said was always correct, but I acquired many a blister trying to prove him right.

We seem to have a devastating effect on seaside piers! The one in Skegness floated away not long after we left and the following summer, we were on stage at the Palace Pier, Brighton for eight weeks and again, not long after our final night, a section of it decided to go for a swim! The Brighton council had the same idea that Skegness had. After years of the old-fashioned show, they decided to go up-market and booked us with Dick Emery, Ken Wood, a wonderful ventriloquist, and three young singing sisters called the Triplets. With such a strong bill the show was bound to succeed and if the theatre had been double the size, it would still have been full.

My first job during summer shows was to find a house to rent. I walked into the first Brighton estate agent's office I could find and met Peter Blackburn, a plumpish man with a twinkle in his eye. Fate must have brought us together because not only did he find me a beautiful home in Saltdean, but he was a good golfer and a member at East Blatchington Golf Club. He organised a seasonal membership for me and we played at least twice a week. During the eight weeks I was in Brighton, we 'halved' many times, but I didn't beat him once.

Peter and I became firm friends partly because we share the same wicked sense of humour and I am proud of the fact that I eventually took his money, on his home course, on my forty-second birthday. His son Anthony also became a great golfer and decided to come into the world of show business. For a while he was entertainments manager of 'Sun City', the now famous South African casino/golf complex. At the present time, he has a management company handling TV presenters and is doing wonderfully well.

# Larry Page

Because EMI had not renewed our recording contract, all interest in making records had disappeared. Money was not a problem, so there was little incentive to continue along those lines. My partners had presumed that the Barron Knights' recording career was over and live work was all that was left.

Although I was still very keen to write a straight hit song, I was finding it difficult having to share my more serious thoughts with comedy ideas for the live show. Having spent most of the day rehearsing and writing, I would then have to switch off, go to my room with the guitar and try to come up with an idea that was romantic. Believe me it was a struggle.

Out of the blue, one day, we had a call from Larry Page who was having enormous success with the Troggs on his Page One label. He'd been given a novelty song with the topical title of *Hey Ho Europe* and thought we would be the ones to put it in the charts for him. Edward Heath was across the Channel every five minutes, at this time, trying to tie up his deal, so it was worth consideration. Although it was a very sub-standard song, I went along to see Larry at his palatial office in Tilney Street, the front door of which was barely a cricket pitch length away from the Dorchester Hotel. Having waited the customary half an hour, I was summoned downstairs to meet him. He wore a sharp suit, a thick gold-banded watch and dark shades over his eyes. Gold records were splashed everywhere and 'Billboard' charts had been framed and had the title of his production underlined on each one. All very impressive!

With his mid-Atlantic accent, he convinced me that *Hey Ho Europe* was going to be a big success and he would do all he could to promote it.

So there I was, faced with a guy offering a record deal

involving a song in which I had no confidence. I went back to talk to Tony and the boys and we decided that because of the position that we were in, we would be foolish to say no.

We cut the track at Pye Studios and it became a dismal flop, but Larry didn't seem to mind. Behind the mask of big-time record producer was a very generous man and he would often ask me out to lunch to discuss any further recording ideas. We always dined at 'Wheelers' fish restaurant before going back to the dungeon to play a few demo's. Like any record company chief, he wanted hits, but he showed an unusual faith in the Barron Knights when others had assumed we were on the recording scrap heap. He begged us to do another parody medley and I had the task of going back to the boys, in the hope that I could twist their arms. Reluctantly, they agreed, and we came up with *Popumentry '71* which involved changing the words to *Banner Man, Did You Ever, Grandad, Chirpy Chirpy Cheep Cheep, The Resurrection Shuffle,* and *Knock Three Times.* As we had had little inspiration floating our way, the resulting medley was unfunny and so Larry had flop number two on his hands.

One day when I was playing him a few songs I had written, he picked out *You're All I Need.* It was a weird track, inspired by the John Kongos hit *He's Gonna Step On You Again.* We went into the Beck Studios, Wellingborough and finished up with a track that had a chance of becoming our first straight hit. Although we were all very pleased with the results, we were surprised that the music press were on our side for a change. Every write-up was positive and Dave Lee Travis gave us a great review on his Radio One show. The sad thing about it was that it became Larry's flop number three! If it had been released under another name, I'm sure it would have been a hit; but we will never know. With no promotion from us and very little marketing, it reached the bottom half of the Canadian and Italian charts!

Larry was not put off. He released two more tracks, *To The Woods* and *Turning My Back On You . . .* Flops four and five!

Radio One just would not play our records. It was so frustrating, but the truth was that the songs were just not up to scratch. So in 1974, when the big hit on the TV was 'Some Mothers Do Have Em', I gave myself a good talking to and wrote *The Ballad Of Frank Spencer*.

It was requested on the 'Stewpot Show' every weekend and we appeared on the Pebble Mill TV show as well as a couple of tea time TV slots. Although the Barron Knights were in high profile for a few weeks, poor Larry still didn't make a cent. However, he still wasn't going to be beaten. Always coming up with ideas, he commissioned Charles Blackwell to write songs for us that would be released under a different name. (Charles had big hits with *Johnny Remember Me*, and *Wild Wind*.)

We were called 'Philly Dog' but we didn't bark very loudly! They were strong songs and we made good sounds, but we felt as if we had entered for the Grand National and could not get over the first jump. However, Larry was still taking me to 'Wheelers' for our fishy lunches and searching for ideas to get our recording career onto the right track.

We hadn't long been back from South Africa, where we had been supporting Petula Clarke and I remembered that her backing vocalists always warmed up with *Danny's Song*, the beautiful track that Kenny Loggins wrote about his brother. I purchased the Loggins and Messina album *Sitting In* and couldn't stop playing that special song; it still is one of my all time favourites. By now, the boys had lost all interest in recording, with the exception of Butch who wrote the occasional song, so when I played *Danny's Song* to Larry, he suggested that I made it a solo single. We had tried everything else, so why not? The boys didn't seem to mind and wished me the best of luck.

Alan Hawkshaw was asked to produce it and between the two of us we achieved a good rapport. I was very pleased with the final mix and proud that my name was on the label but I prayed for Larry's sake, as well as mine, that it would be a hit.

While on my way to Lyndrick golf course near Worksop, listening to my car radio, I heard Tony Blackburn announce, 'And here's a brand new artiste, Pete Langford singing *Danny's Song*.' I had a good chuckle to myself and at the same time was very surprised at how good it sounded. I was even more surprised when it came to the end and he said, 'I like that so much I'm gonna play it again.'

Could this be the hit for which Larry had tried so hard, or was I asking too much? . . . I'm afraid I was. Like *The Ballad Of Frank Spencer*, it was a turntable hit, and they make you no money.

Selling our cover albums after the shows in all the big cabaret clubs was proving to be a good money maker and we would sell over two hundred a night. Their contents were basically the hits of the day and while not very inspiring, the profits were good!

We eventually parted from Larry, but still kept in touch. He's one of those guys who could pop up at any time and surprise us all with a monster hit. I went on to reach great heights with my song-writing! I wrote the theme tune for the Luton Town Football Club *Hatters Hatters*. I watch them once a year, when thay play against Spurs and if it's played over the tannoy, I sink to the ground!

## Les Perrin

If you have a good publicity man, you can just sit back and look at the pictures! We had the best there was in Les Perrin. He handled the Dave Clarke Five, the Rolling Stones and us. We monopolised the front pages of the Daily Sketch and Daily

Mirror on several occasions, but mainly because of events such as weddings and new babies, etc.

During the press call for the Summer show in Brighton, most of the reporters and photographers were around Dick Emery, so Les advised us to keep out of the way until they had exhausted their supply of questions. Then at the right moment, he grabbed one of the dancing girls, which just happened to be the one with the biggest boobs, and we picked her up and laid her horizontally across our arms. The photographers flashed through a reel of film each and the next morning we were all over the front pages! Unfortunately, all that poor old Dick got was a mention in our write-up. That's just one example of Les's skill.

In 1971, the Australian authorities lifted the entry ban on the Rolling Stones, which they'd imposed because of their earlier drug problems. Les decided to go to Sydney two weeks ahead of the Stones, so as to hopefully calm the media down and correct a few wrong assumptions. He knew that we were in town, so he asked Tony and Butch to meet him at the airport.

The aircraft landed at 7 am and in the Customs Hall Les answered all the necessary questions, but as soon as they knew who he was, they whisked him away and subjected him to a tough grilling; they even stripped him naked, in spite of the fact that he was very frail and suffering with an illness from which he had only a slim chance of recovery. The actions of the Australian Customs Officers did little to improve his health! After waiting several hours, Butch had to leave for the show, so Tony remained alone, waiting for Les. He eventually came through the Arrivals door and Tony then had to rush him to the TV station, where he was scheduled for an interview.

Les explained to the interviewer what kind of day he had had and that he was totally exhausted, so please, no questions about the drugs; another interview would be granted to answer any question asked on this subject. This was agreed; on came the red light and the first question was, 'Mr Perrin, tell me the latest news on the drug problems that the Rolling Stones have?' Les was in a virtual state of collapse but managed to answer with dignity. He was a gentleman to the end and Fleet Street missed him very much.

# South Africa

In January, 1974, we flew to Cape Town to begin a three week tour of South Africa supporting Petula Clarke. It's always very pleasant to leave the cold and damp British winter and to arrive in a country that's enjoying hot sunshine.

We were met by Dave Yelland, an Afrikaan, who wasted no time in telling a nearby black fellow to put all our cases in the truck and deliver them to the hotel. He spoke to him as though he was a savage animal and we were all taken aback by the whole incident. When we arrived at the hotel, we listened as the tough Mr Yelland gave the black guy another verbal bashing. It didn't set the tone for a happy relationship with our Dutch lump of a tour manager!

Having settled into our rooms, we all went to the bar to meet a reporter and almost the first thing he said was that we should ignore the fact that the whites treated the blacks like slaves, that the blacks were very grateful to have a job and were used to being told what to do rather than be asked. Although we found it most disturbing, we were guests in another country and had to tolerate all that was around us. The blacks had their own buses, their own seats in the park, and their own little spot on the beaches. It was difficult to ignore it all.

To see the sun in January was such a treat and we wasted very little time in exposing our lily-white bodies to that powerful blob in the sky! We suffered badly as a result of our exposure and could be seen that night in the bar, walking around like tightly bandaged mummies. Needless to say, the sun had burned us all rather badly.

Lennie Bennett, the comedian in this show, had brought his wife Margaret, a buxom blonde from Blackpool with that typical Northern warmth and very proud of her home town.

One morning, she was stretched out on the sunbed by the poolside. It was a beautiful day; blue sky and a light breeze swaying the palm trees. We had just finished the most exotic breakfast consisting of all the local fresh fruits and anything on toast served at your poolside table.

'Hey, Margaret,' I said, 'it's a bit better than Blackpool isn't it?'

'You've got to be bloody joking,' she replied in a very angry voice, 'Blackpool's much better than this place because the air is more bracing.' I thought she was winding me up, so I began to laugh.

'I'm bloody serious,' she said. 'The beaches at Blackpool are much bigger and there are definitely more fish and chip shops!'

The opening night at the Three Arts Theatre was a wonderful success and made really special by the fact that the audience came dressed for the occasion, something we hadn't been used to. The ladies were elegant in their long dresses, while the men wore bow ties. Lennie opened the show, followed by the Perrards, a tumbling duo from Adelaide. We closed the first half and Petula performed for the whole of the second half. The entire show had been booked by Selwyn Miller, a local agent, who was working for the Quibell brothers, again a local family, who had put on shows in Cape Town for many years.

One Sunday afternoon, we were all invited to a picnic at the Quibell house, which was surrounded by fifteen acres of

*Johannesburg, 1974. Rolf had a new cine camera and tested it on my poor acrobatics.*

beautiful gardens with a pool, tennis court and a cricket pitch. We hadn't seen such opulence before. Everything was on a massive scale, even down to the opposition's score, when they beat us in the three hour test match! Butch was the only one on our side to score any runs.

We eventually had to leave beautiful Cape Town for the more industrial Johannesburg. Dave Yelland had insisted, before we left, that all the baggage should be in two groups; red tape had to be stuck on all the cases that were for the show and the personal luggage that we needed at the hotel had to have yellow tape. This little job was given to the wide-eyed and very scared, black lad.

The Llandrost Hotel was our home for the week in Jo'burg. It was without doubt the most luxurious place in which we'd ever stayed. It was part of the Southern Sun chain owned by Sol Kurzner, the man responsible for 'Sun City'. Harry Murray, the English manager, was most helpful to his visitors from home and he arranged a trip down a gold mine and more important to me, golf at the Royal Jo'burg course.

The day we spent at the gold mine was most interesting. Our guided tour began in a classroom, where we stood at the back and listened to a white teacher giving lessons in mine language. This was a combination of signs and words that were unique to the goldmines around South Africa. It had been devised as the quickest way to teach the blacks, who came straight from their tribal village to earn money to be sent home to their families. I was suprised at how clean the mine itself was. Even a mile below the surface, there wasn't a speck of dust to be seen, until you arrived at the point where the workers were drilling holes for the explosives. How different to the Welsh coal mine, where within minutes of descending, we were covered in black dust and had sore eyes for days afterwards.

The distance between the Colossium Theatre and the Llandrost Hotel was a mere short walk, but we always took the transport provided, as, when dusk fell, Jo'burg wasn't the safest place for a peaceful walk and a touch of window shopping. The theatre was a very old, traditional building, ready for refurbishment and caused me some anxiety with regard to the volume of my guitar. I could just imagine the vibration bringing a lump of plaster off the ceiling and crashing onto the heads of the middle row of the stalls!

As the rand was very weak against the pound, most things were cheap to buy, especially booze. The boys had taken a fancy to Lion beer and I was very partial to a glass of cold, dry white wine. It was quite usual for us to have a morning sunbathe, then sit under the umbrella and have lunchtime drinks before going to our room for a rest before the show. This particular lunchtime, I'm afraid we abused the brain cells and had one, possibly two, too many! Barron was the first to leave the little party and wander back to his room. Five minutes later, we heard shouting coming from his balcony. When we looked up, there was Barron in his swimming trunks, telling us that he was going to jump from his third floor 'diving board'. Before we could tell him he was mad, there was a big splash! As he climbed out of the water, he said, 'I do sincerely apologise, I am now going to sleep,' and off he trotted through the glass doors. His behaviour was so out of character, that I really thought that he'd been having a puff of that leafy substance that makes you feel high. There was plenty of it around. Each time I played golf, the black caddies would hand me a little rolled up package and say, 'You smoke grass Boss, this cheap, make you randy.'

Jo'burg was supporting two shows that week, ours and the Rolf Harris Show. We hadn't seen him since the Beatles tour so we had plenty of news to catch up on. Every morning he would come into 'Omah's Kitchen', the twenty-four hour bistro in the hotel, where together, we would sing some very complicated harmony songs.

Rolf, although to this day he doesn't know it, was responsible for a re-occurrence of my back trouble. Sol Kurzner had invited the casts of the Petula Clarke and Rolf Harris shows to his beautiful home for a barbecue. Again, like the Quibell's house, it was set in large grounds with a pool and anything else you could think of, including a trampoline. Rolf had just purchased a new cine camera and after spending most of the afternoon reading the instructions, he began to film a few magic moments and asked me to start jumping up and down on the trampoline. I've never been one to hold back on any challenge, but never having had any previous experience on a trampoline, I didn't know what to expect. I was begining to reach a good height with my jumps, when he asked me to do a summersault and I didn't give it a second thought. Over I went, executed a perfect twist, and landed flat on my back. Rolf said, 'Cheers mate,' in his Aussie drawl and I stepped off the apparatus, feeling very pleased with myself. Ten minutes later I was frozen to my chair; my back had 'gone' in exactly the same place as before! Next day, I was in the hotel gym, having treatment.

Butch also had a painful time while trying some silly exercise. The Llandrost physical training instructor was putting him through his paces one morning, when an overstretch made him yell. The instructor thought Butch had slipped a disc and fancying himself as a chiropractor, he laid Butch down, cracked a few of his bones and . . . made him worse!

For the next few days, the two of us were walking around with a limp and a stoop and our signature tune became, *Bend Me, Shape Me*. Having so much fun, we forgot our aches and pains until one morning, when we were stunned by some very sad news from home. We were all gathering in reception but Barron, militarily strict with his timekeeping, was unusually late. At last, we saw the lift doors open and he walked out, looking very pale. He quietly told us that his brother-in-law had been killed in a car crash. He'd apparently driven out from his local pub and lost control on a bend before hitting a bridge. Seaton was a close friend of us all who only a few weeks before, had been to our house to try and sell the Mercedes that he had been driving the day he crashed.

The last week of the tour was spent in Durban. The City Hall, the only place that could accommodate a big show, was an awful place for sound control. If you stamped your foot, the whole population of Durban got up and danced! I was greeted at the hotel in Durban, by a friend that I had met at the British Open Golf Championship when it was played at Troon, in Scotland. Maurice Bembridge, the ex-Ryder Cup player, had then introduced me to Doug Cox. His lined face made him look older than he was and there was more fat to be found on a starving sparrow! He had two sets of golf clubs in the boot of his car, so off we drove to the Royal Durban Golf Club. When we arrived there, he placed a white tin, marked with a red cross, inside his golf bag and when curiosity got the better of me and I enquired about the tin, he opened it up to reveal syringes: to be used in case of snake bites. If he was trying to frighten me, it worked. I don't think I hit into the rough at all that day. We did see a snake curled around a tree as we were crossing a bridge, but Doug insisted that we should keep walking as normal. Apparently, it was a Green Mamber and very poisonous, so there was no danger of me stopping to have a friendly chat. Arriving at a par three hole, we found that the green was full of monkeys, at least twenty of them, some with babies clinging to their bellies. Doug said, 'Just hit the ball, Pete, you will miss them all.'

I did and they didn't even flinch. Doug did the same and they still stayed rooted to the spot. Then they cleared the green when we went to putt out and returned to their positions again as soon as we walked away. Doug later told me that there were more hole-in-one's recorded on that hole than bruised monkey heads.

Unfortunately, Doug is no longer with us. He died shortly after the tour, but not from a snake bite; he smoked too many ciggies!

We decided that the last day of the tour should be one to be remembered. We'd had enough of Dave Yelland shouting at the blacks, so we came up with a scheme to give him something to shout about. Lennie Bennett rang down to the hotel reception and in a clipped, loud, South African accent, he shouted, 'Hello, it's Dave Yelland here. I'm on my way to the airport and I have to catch the next flight to Cape Town. Can you go to my room and pack my case, then deliver it to the airport, where I will be waiting at the check-in desk.'

We will never know to this day what he said when he next went to his room and found his belongings missing.

Part of Petula's act was a medley of songs from *Jesus Christ, Superstar*. Her presentation of this section can only be described as quite dramatic. The orchestra would strike up the intro to the tune of the title track, then it would stop, leaving only Kenny Clayton on piano. Petula then turned her back on the audience, walked towards the piano, dropped her head into the palms of her hands and looked into the piano. After a few seconds of silence, she then sang, 'I don't know how to love him', etc. It must have looked cool from the front and was, without doubt, the most impressive part of her show.

Down to the joke shop we went and purchased the most perfect-looking dog turd you ever did see. We placed it in the open grand piano and watched her final performance in Durban. The orchestra hit the intro, she did the big turn around, looked into the piano and said into the microphone, 'Jesus Christ!'

The audience howled with laughter as we, led by her husband Claude Woolfe, danced the Can Can across the stage.

Many a female act would have been most upset with our schoolboy pranks, but she took it all in good spirit and carried on with the rest of the show. We knew we had to leave it there.

*Dave Yelland, bottom centre, insisting we wear identification tape. Top left is Lennie Bennett. Claude Wolff, top right. South Africa.*

All the shows in South Africa were for whites only, with the exception of one. This was the show where Butch, for the first time in his life, failed to get a laugh with a comment that was a certain 'Whoofer' anywhere else.

For years he's always introduced me as the negative for the golliwog on the jam jar and without thinking, he said the same that night to a theatre full of blacks. There was an awful silence that lasted three seconds, but seemed like a lifetime. Lennie was busting his sides in the wings but all Butch wanted was a big hole to swallow him up.

We all enjoyed South Africa so much and would have often gone back there if politics hadn't stood in our way. I will never understand the reasons why they banned musicians, entertainers and sportsmen, from working in South Africa. They are the people who are trained to give pleasure to the masses. It's frowned upon if we set foot in that beautiful country to work; but, if we were trained to kill and were funded by the government of the day, we could waltz through any passport control.

I want to go back, if only to find out if Dave Yelland ever retrieved his case and to stand on that tee at Royal Durban and try to give a monkey a headache; but most of all, to perform in front of a mixed-race audience.

# Golf

1975/76 were the two years I disliked the most. The Barron Knights were going nowhere, except up and down the M1. We had a system of working a week on and a week off and although there were enough nightclubs to work fifty-two weeks a year, none of us wanted that. There was still no sign of a recording contract simply because we hadn't written anything to warrant one. Our financial situation was still very good and improving; consequently, there was no pressure on us to do anything more than put on our stage suits, get in front of the audience and make them laugh.

Butch and I were becoming golf fanatics and most mornings, when we were away from home, we would head for the nearest golf course and challenge anyone who fancied their chances. After seasons at Blackpool, Skegness and Brighton, I played a reasonable game off a nine handicap and Butch was very handy with fourteen shots to play around with.

Whenever we were in the Stockton–Darlington area, we would always head for Dinsdale Spar Golf Club. Ray Steele, the resident professional, kept an eye on our swings and often sent us out to play with a couple of locals, who didn't mind parting with their money. His two small sons, David and Graham, were very handy players, as was his wife, Joan. David eventually became a professional himself, before settling down on the Costa Del Sol selling golf carts.

One spring morning at Dinsdale, I was on the par three 7th and hit a shot that landed on the green and bounced into the hedge behind. We went in search of the ball and found the clever little thing resting in a birds nest, keeping three green speckled eggs company. Not one of them was damaged. If I'd had a camera and photographed this little miracle, who would have believed me?

A week later, in the Daily Mirror, there was a picture of a golf ball sitting in a birds' nest, with the caption, 'A real birdie!' Someone had hit it there and, guess what, they also had a camera in their pocket. Well bless my soul!

Hedley Muscroft, the professional at Roundhay in Leeds, always made the two of us welcome, mainly because he loved to get us on the course and empty our wallets. We got wise to some of his gamesmanship, but not without learning the hard way. He and his assistant, Eddie Bullock, used to let us win the first two holes and then wanted to double the stakes and start a fresh game. By the time we'd arrived at the eighteenth hole, there were about six games going on! We'd lost five and needed to chip in, to save losing a few bob on the last game.

If ever there was a time when it looked as though we were on a winning streak, he would say, 'Hey Pete, you're playing great today, you're using your legs so well.' Another gem he would use was, 'What a great position you get to, at the top.'

You then spent the next few holes thinking about how good your legs were and how wonderful you must look at the top of your swing, but the one thing you forgot altogether was how to hit the ball. Butch and I survived all the banter and eventually took them both to the cleaners, which really upset Hedley, until we agreed to spend the money we'd won in the pro shop! Roundhay was the first and only course where I shot a gross 69.

Butch and I christened ourselves Smith and Jones. We were very hard to beat and were becoming bandits off our handicaps. Mind you, we had learned a few choice remarks from Hedley and we could take a few without being affected. The pro that gave us the most 'verbal' was Peter Stebbings. We first met him at the Hillside Club in Southport and he went on to be the official starter for the PGA, before settling at Lostock Golf Club, near Bolton.

The first remark he ever made to me, on our first game, was, 'I hope you filled your car up before you got here, because you'll be broke when you leave.'

We had a few battles, but none better than when Butch and I took Pete and his best friend David Whittaker on, at the famous Royal Lytham Golf Club. We had a trophy made and we hyped-up the match to give them the impression that it was more than just a 'friendly'. As soon as we walked on to the first tee, a 170 yd, par three, Pete started all the chat, 'You'll need two good shots to get on here, Langford.'

I hit a 4 iron on to the green and sunk the putt to go one up and replied, 'You were perfectly right, Pete. It's two good shots.'

Butch and I were a good team that day. He played very steadily and if he faltered, I was there to keep us in front. When we walked up the 17th fairway, we were one up and three of us got onto the green in two, but Whittaker hit the greenside bunker and ended up with a five. Butch and I both managed our par fours, so the heat was on. Pete had to two-putt to keep the game alive and his first putt was a good one, ending up about 12 inches from the hole. He was about to pick it up, thinking we had conceded but I asked him to finish it off. As he looked at me 'daggers', I told him it was a crucial part of the game and no 'gimmies' were allowed at this stage. As he was bending over his putter and preparing to hit, I could see the Red Arrows in the distance, high in the sky, although you couldn't hear them. I said, 'Look, there's the Red Arrows.' Pete went crazy, but realised I was telling the truth. He again lined up his very short putt, but took a day and age to hit it, and . . . he missed.

Whittaker hit the roof and called Pete all sorts of names that I can't print. Pete himself, went very pale; it had to be the shortest putt he'd ever missed. We won the trophy, along with a shilling or two, but Whittaker had the last touch of glory. In a temper, he drove his ball out of sight on the last hole and sunk an eight iron for an eagle two! Apparently, on the journey back to Bolton poor Pete went through hell!

Pete now has his own driving range in North Wales and David Whittaker still runs the family department store in Bolton.

Having played soccer, cricket, squash and many other sports, I find that golf has many qualities that make it special above all others. I've made many friends around the world through golf and when you're away from home, it's great to pop up to the local club and see if there is a game going. The clubs are usually in the best part of town and when the game is over, you shake hands, win or lose, go for a quiet beer and talk about 'if only'. It took me 29 years to achieve a 'hole in one', an 8 iron to the 145 yd eleventh at Torquay Golf Club in August 1993.

Although I was playing golf three or four times a week, I was still very much occupied with writing and had two singles released which were performed by other acts. John Farrah's wife, Pat, recorded *Leave My Love In Your Old Backyard*, which was released in the States and 'Brother Kip', a black band from Letchworth recorded *Super Da Day*, an attempt at reggae. Neither of them became a hit, but at least I was proud of the songs. I also had a good time producing three good tracks for the Batchelors, including finding the best songs and using the best musicians. It made me realise how much there was to learn about finding the right 'chemistry' for a hit.

In the meantime, the Barron Knights had recorded two excellent tracks, *Put Yourself In My Place* and *Hooks Out Of You*. It rekindled the boys' thoughts about recording and we felt very confident that they would become hits, but the response from the record companies was, 'It's not funny!'

# C.S.E.

Combined Services Entertainment is an organisation designed to cheer up the troops in any part of the world. Wherever there is trouble, or a British stronghold to be protected, you will find the Army, Navy or Air Force in residence and, more often than not, without the normal luxury of being able to pop down the road to see a live show. That's where CSE comes in. It is a government-funded agency for the troops.

In 1974, we were asked, by the CSE, to go to Cyprus, accompanied by Lois Lane, a singing trio called the New Faces, and comedian Johnny Hackett. Representing CSE as tour manager was Derek Agguter, father of actress Jenny. He was an ex-officer and still retained his wide military stride and affinity for the taste for alchohol.

Famagusta was the first venue in line for the show. It was a three-hour coach drive from the airport, but as the first night was free, there was no particular rush. Within an hour of starting the coach journey, Derek wanted to stop at a Taverna to welcome the cast and musicians in the show to the island. This idea was greeted with much enthusiasm and within minutes, the fourteen of us were sitting at a long table with the wine and the beer flowing and our voices slowly rising from loud to a deafening roar. The only thing missing was the food. Derek had told the waiter to bring a mixture for all to sample at our leisure, but the chef obviously wanted us to be so hungry that whatever he dished up, we would have thought it came from the Ritz.

With the combination of too much booze and our bellies full of Greek food, we all climbed back onto the coach. Derek sat in the front seat next to the driver and fell asleep before the engine was switched on, while the rest of us started the community singing. We were happily into the dirty section of *Old King Cole*, when we noticed that the outside of the windows looked as if they had been fired at by a cannon loaded with rice pudding. In actual fact, it was Derek with his head out of the window at seventy miles an hour, unloading a few stuffed vine leaves and, with the help of the wind, had decorated the whole length of the coach!

John Porter, our piano accompanist for the show, was lying

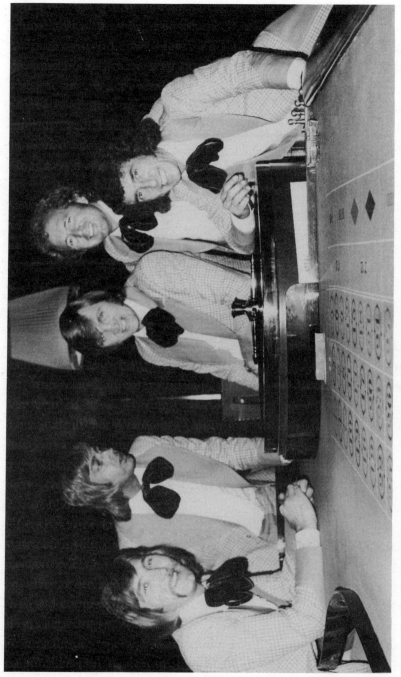

*Were our bow ties really that big?*

along the back seat complaining that there was no beer on the coach, but he had almost drunk Cyprus dry in a very short space of time. When we reached the hotel entrance, John was the first one to get off the coach, which had stopped by a very large fishpond in front of half a dozen steps leading to the big glass double doors. He then walked straight through the fish pond, up the steps, pushed open the doors and proceeded to take down his soaking wet trousers. He handed them to the receptionist and in his very deep voice demanded that they be cleaned ready for the morning. He then disappeared and was not seen again until an hour before the show the following day.

After only a few days in Cyprus, we realised that CSE tours were a good excuse for a piss-up. The Government provided booze at lunch, dinner, pre-show and afterwards, when we were always invited back to the officers' mess for even more food and . . . booze.

We paid many visits to Gibraltar, where all the shows were held at Inces Hall. We always performed on three nights: one show each for the Army, Navy and RAF. On the first night, the Brigadier was in the front row, wearing a black patch over one eye. In the officers' mess afterwards, he approached all of us, one by one, and repeated about ten times, 'Wonderful show! Mind you, I only saw half of it, ha ha.' His wife came up with an original compliment, 'I thoroughly enjoyed your noises,' she said. We think that was one of the nicest put-downs and spoken with such subtlety.

During the Falklands War CSE took many shows, consisting mainly of dancing girls and a comedian, down to the South Atlantic. Although we were asked on numerous occasions, we were always faced with the problem of transporting our sound system. Eventually, a compromise was reached and we went as far as Ascension Island, which is the halfway station for all the comings and goings. It's a volcanic island that lies between South America and South Africa. Because it is volcanic, Ascension is a very dark, grey island with the exception of Green Mountain, so-called simply because it has a green peak. The road winds up the mountain to its destination, the Red Lion pub, a little stone building sitting in the middle of a few acres of vegetable gardens, that spend most of their time in cloud; hence the green vegetation. The whole area is populated by folks from Tristan da Cunha, an island previously devastated by an erupting volcano.

On our first visit, we were looked after by the squadron that was responsible for in-flight refuelling. They had their own DIY miniature village, complete with bar! We slept on mattresses in tiny dusty huts and a ten-minute walk away from these were the ablutions, where there were two toilets to choose from, the English or the American. The English one had the usual stand-ups for peeing, but for dumping, you had a choice of an open row of sit-downs. It wasn't easy sitting next to a soldier with your pants down below your knees, while he was insisting that he saw us on Crackerjack when he was a little boy! The American bog was one of splendour! The showers were individual cubicles, as were the loos for your big jobs and although we were not officially allowed to use them, we found it fairly easy to go through their doors by adopting an American accent!

Our second visit, two years later, was a much more luxurious affair. With Dave Lee, the comedian for the show, the tour manager and our road manager Doug, we had the right number of people for two huts with four people in each. A swimming pool had been built and with the British having claimed a victory in the war, the atmosphere was more like a holiday camp. One day, we were all invited to go big game fishing, when each of us took a turn in trying to catch a Tuna or Dolphin fish. The sea was teeming with fish, so the boat was much heavier on its return to the dock and after saving enough for a barbecue on the beach, we gave the rest of our catch to the

*Preparing for a helicopter trip around Ascension Island, South Atlantic.*

*CSE tour. Munchengladbach, Germany, 1969. Dick Emery, centre. Peter Goodwright, front, second from left.*

121

locals. We had taken lunch on an oil tanker, moored a mile off-shore and been given a helicopter ride around Green Mountain, in addition to all the other enjoyable experiences and so it was hard to leave our 'Butlins' in the South Atlantic.

Our last visit to Cyprus was in 1987 and it proved to be a painful trip for me. Our support in the show was a stage version of 'A Question of Sport', with Ralph Dellor as the question master and Emlyn Hughes, boxer John H. Stracy and water ski champion Liz Hobbs included in the teams.

Emlyn and John were so competitive that they would set up sporty games all through the day! There would be swimming, football against the waiters, table tennis and even the dreaded golf. The three of us were playing on a course that had 'browns' rather than greens; these were formed with rolled sand, topped with oil, which formed a good putting surface. Massive chunks of rock were also littered around the course and it was one of these which proved to be my downfall that day! We were playing the seventeenth and my drive had hit the rough. I smashed the ball out with a four iron and it flew out a treat; but it struck a boulder about twenty yards in front of me and rebounded straight onto the bone above my eye.

For a few moments, I saw stars! There was blood everywhere and Emlyn rushed to my assistance. We hurried to the little club house, where the barman put me in his car and took me to the military hospital. They sewed me up with six stitches and advised me on how to hit a four iron!

I don't think there is another group in the UK that has performed more shows for the troops than the Barron Knights. There will always tend to be a lack of facilities on these trips and other problems to overcome, but all the folks on the tour are ready to muck in and make the few days very enjoyable. It's not unusual to arrive at a venue, only to find that there is no staging or even electricity. This happened to us in

Munchengladbach, Germany, when, in mid-winter we were due to perform a show in an aircraft hanger. When we arrived, it was deserted; no chairs for the audience, no light, nothing, but within the hour, two lorries pulled up, out jumped a dozen soldiers and the big, empty space was transformed into a replica of Earls Court!

It will always be a pleasure to continue to entertain the troops.

## *The Comeback Year*

1977 began with a two-week trip to Rhodesia. We took Manchester comic Ven Tracy with us and a boy and girl singing duo called the Voyagers. When we opened in Salisbury on the 3rd January to a packed house, we found it amazing that so many people had heard of us in this part of Africa. The whites and blacks seemed to get along fine there, which made us feel safer and made for a better atmosphere.

On our many trips abroad, we always tried to organise 'group outings', as we did when we visited the gold mine and went on a safari in Krugersdorf National Park, so after making a few enquiries and acquiring a couple of complimentary tickets, we found ourselves setting out to visit a tobacco farm. Anticipating a long day out in the Rhodesian countryside, we were disappointed at how long it took us to get there. When we eventually arrived, we were greeted by the owners of the farm who told us that they grew the Golden Virginia leaf. We just had time to run around the drying sheds, have a beer, then climb back into the VW combi to race back to the Jameson Hotel for a clean up. We made the show just in time. I did however, manage to take pictures to remind myself that I did go!

After a sell-out week in Salisbury, we headed for Bulawayo to do the same. I just wish that we could have made it an annual trip, but again the politicians stood in the way.

To have the sun on your back in January is always a nice experience and being paid to work in the sunshine is even better. After seeing all the happy, smiling faces in the sunshine, I've always found it hard to return to England in mid-winter, where it's gloomy and colourless with that low, cold, misty cloud that makes everybody walk around with a long face. But the family reunion at Heathrow Airport makes up for it all!

After sunshine, good, well-presented food and the smart hotels of Salisbury, Rhodesia, we found ourselves at the High Post Hotel seven miles north of Salisbury, Wiltshire. From the outside, it looked like something that the Germans had bombed and the local council couldn't be bothered to rebuild! The inside was even worse: wallpaper was peeling off the wall in my bedroom and there was no heating at all, except from the hot water tap in the permanently stained sink. We watched a mouse run over the buffet and ran a competition to spot the drinking glass without lipstick on the rim.

Alan, the hotel manager/receptionist/cook/compère wore milk-bottle-bottomed glasses and a tilted toupé. From morning till night, he was permanently dressed in a black suit, white shirt and black dickie bow. His collar was always bloodstained from standing too close to the razor and the button above his waist belt was always undone because of his beer belly, and I mustn't forget the food stains on his jacket!

The hotel was called the High Post for obvious reasons. It

was perched on the top of the hill between Salisbury and Amesbury, where the February wind blew cold. The function room held about four hundred people, but I couldn't believe that they came in their coach-loads to this tumble-down, odd piece of architecture.

When Alan became compère for the night, there was no peace and quiet for the patrons. He would speak into the microphone every five minutes to tell them who was coming next, what else was on the menu and if the sun was going to shine in Omsk! He stepped off the stage one night, to welcome a party that was celebrating a couple's wedding anniversary.

'How long have you been married?' he asked in a strong Wiltshire accent.

'Twenty-eight years,' the woman replied.

'Any kids?' he asked.

'Five,' she said, slightly embarrassed.

'Five?' he blurted, 'you dirty cow.'

I must take a drive to that area one day, in the hope that the High Post has been demolished at last and replaced by a 'Toys R Us'. It did have one good point though, a golf course across the road.

There's something I find hard to understand about us English. When I've been away on a Mediterranean holiday or even a ski trip to the Alps, the people who complain the most about the food and service are, without doubt, the British. Yet put us back into our own country and we put up with the worst service and standard of food that you can find in the whole of Europe. Spending most of our lives in hotels, as we do, I only wish I could say that we compare favourably to anywhere in the world, but we fall short by a long way. One of life's pleasures is going out to a smart restaurant and having a good waiter serve cuisine that is satisfying. It's common everywhere, except in dear old Great Britain.

However it does bring out the flavour for a chuckle.

In a certain four-star hotel in Nottingham, a little nervous, Oriental girl came to the table to take my breakfast order. I requested my usual poached egg on brown toast and because I never seem to get brown toast, I made a point of emphasising the 'brown toast'. Sure enough, ten minutes later, little Miss Suzi Wong placed in front of me poached egg on white toast. I said, 'Excuse me, I did ask for brown toast.' She gave me a big smile and a squint before saying, 'Oh, I'm sorry sir, you want it done a little bit more?'

Cooking and serving food is an art form. I love to watch a chef prepare a meal and to see a top Italian or French waiter glide around a table, with his spoon and fork in one hand and the silver dish in the other. It will always be a good enough reason to leave a little gratuity!

Paris House, in the grounds of Woburn Abbey, Bedfordshire, is run by Peter Chandler, one of the best chefs to come out of the Roux Brothers' 'stable'. His food is exquisite and Veronica was lucky enough to spend some time in the kitchens of this beautiful place, and having attended a Chefs' Course, she has become a superb cook. Why I'm not a fatty I will never know, but I do get spoiled when meal time comes around. I've promised myself that one day I will return the service. At the moment Indian Chicken Do-Piaza is the only meal I have managed to conquer!

The cabaret clubs were still going through a very lucrative period and any person who wanted to be in show business would soon find a job. The biggest crowd-pullers were Bob Monkhouse and ourselves and if there was anyone bigger, they wouldn't work in the same places, anyway. It wasn't my favourite type of work as it meant going on stage at 11 pm, when most people are thinking of going to bed and the audience, by that time, are full of alchohol mixed with chicken and chips! We've sung in some of the most exotic nightclubs in the world, like Tito's in Palma, Majorca, Sam Lord's Castle in Barbados and a season at the historic Talk of the Town in London, but for me, a theatre is the place to learn the true craft of entertaining; that's where you can work and create a routine from nothing to success. In a night club, you must work from a very tight base or you will find the audience will just start mumbling!

After the 'wonderfully luxurious' few days in Salisbury, Wiltshire, we worked 'back-to-back' weeks in Caerphilly, Brighton, Bedford and Watford and I was ready for a good holiday with Veronica and Tanya. We flew to Los Angeles and introduced Tanya to Disneyland and Universal Studios before driving to Las Vegas to see how the Americans put on a live show. Much to Tanya's approval, we saw the Osmonds at the Hilton, where the food and service were faultless and the show was so good, I felt like phoning England and asking the boys to get over to Vegas quickly and see how it should be done. So much care had been taken over every detail as well as the lighting and sound, but most impressive of all was the excitement generated by the performers. It made me realise just how complacent we had become, with the result that our show had fallen behind the times, for example, our show was forty-five minutes long and we refused to do any longer!

While I was in the States, I had this one thought that really struck home! I had seen all the big stars appear on the Johnny Carson Show and endless other chat shows and had seen their names in lights in Las Vegas and they were all recording stars, who still depended on having hit records. They seemed to keep the momentum of their success going and although I tried hard to do the same with the lads, I had problems in getting my point across without upsetting one or two of them. As a rule, we had no obvious conflict or argument between us, but there was definitely a 'them and me' situation when it came to making records. Butch was the only one who really understood what I was trying to do and it took me a long while to fathom out why there was so little interest from the rest.

Butch, like me, is a Rock'n'Roller; we were brought up on the great songs that excited and inspired you. He's an excellent musician with a great feel for chord changes and rhythm. When I first met Barron and Dave, they were Jazzers and the one thing they didn't have was a natural feel for rhythm. They would be the first to admit that they were not too good on their chosen instruments, so their love of music wasn't so deep. Duke wasn't, and still isn't a player. In his early days, he was a Ray Charles fanatic and would rather listen to music than write it. So for three of the guys, recording was a chore and gave them no pleasure.

Summer 1977 was no different from the previous five and the locations were not that inspiring either. However, weeks in Sheffield, Batley, Cleethorpes, Nottingham, Stoke and Eccles all helped us to keep our wallets fat and to own good homes and new cars.

On Sunday, the 14th August, we played to two full houses at the Festival Theatre, Paignton and in the audience were Tommy Steele and Lennie Bennett, who invited us back to their hotel for a drink after the show. I had met Tommy on a few occasions in Blackpool, when we had both been working there and he had often asked me to play in his showbiz football team. Why he asked me is a mystery, as I was a 9st 7lb, left-footed, afraid-to-tackle player, but always keen to make up the numbers.

After a couple of drinks and a few jokes from Lennie, Tommy and I finished the evening in deep conversation about the future of the Barron Knights. He advised me that in order to keep the fans with us, we had to maintain a high standard of performance and material in our show and he also considered that we would be mad not to work hard on another record similar to our past hits. We had created our Image and we would never lose it!

The very next day we drove to Tenby, South Wales and during that six hour journey there was no idle chat! Barron and I got into a very heated discussion about our future recording plans. He and Duke were definitely against any form of comedy medley; Dave didn't mind one way or the other as his main interests were outside of the Barron Knights, but Butch, as always, was there to support me!

After the beautiful Festival Theatre in Paignton, the Tenby venue was a depressing sight. A dance hall with no stage and a few tables and chairs down both sides. Brixton Prison canteen would have had more atmosphere! Four days of misery were ahead of us and just to prove that the management hadn't a clue how to run the place, we performed the opening night with the house lights permanently up!

When we were away from home, it was customary for us to meet after breakfast each morning, usually to discuss what had gone wrong the night before. We would be very frank with each other, which resulted in a better performance at the next show.

At that time there were two sections of our show which were more outstanding, mainly because they'd been born of fresh ideas. The second song of the perfomance was a very funny rewrite of *Float On* by the Floaters, which we presented with all the twists and turns associated with the American black groups. As a finale, when we did the medley of the hits, we substituted new lyrics to Leo Sayer's *You Make Me Feel Like Dancing*. Both were good examples of strong Barron Knights writing.

At this particular after-breakfast meeting, Butch had sung to us the new words he had written to the Brotherhood of Man hit *Angelo*.

We roared with laughter, then went straight to the hall, sat in the dressing room upstairs and rehearsed it for the show that night. We had to convince Butch that the name Ivanhoe should be changed to Walthamstow in the new verse, as not many people would have heard of the tiny village in Buckinghamshire. That night, it didn't get quite the reaction that we were expecting, but because *Angelo* had made number one the previous month, we decided to keep it in, as it was new material for our routine.

After the morning rehearsal, Barron and I went back to the hotel for a coffee and I continued to try and convince him that we had good fodder for another hit record. Again the conversation began to get heated, so in the end, I told him that I would record it, pay for it and reap the rewards. Feeling annoyed that I had not been more diplomatic, I just walked away from him, knowing that he was thinking what an arsehole I was, but I felt very confident that he would come round to my way of thinking.

Just talking about it wasn't enough, I had to put the whole concept together and present it in a form ready to record. Because I was so determined, I found the writing easy and before the night was out, I'd committed to paper all the incidental music that knitted the medley together and given the whole thing the title of *Live in Trouble*.

After the show on the Tuesday, I went from the dressing-room straight to the hotel to double check that I was completely satisfied with my creation! I was more than excited about the whole idea. I made myself a coffee, switched on the radio above my bed and within seconds heard a news flash . . . Elvis was dead!

My first reaction was to ring Veronica and she, like the whole world, was on the verge of tears. I then went to find the boys in the bar and for the next two hours we had our own wake!

On Monday, 22nd August, we began a week's work at the Crystal Rooms, Hereford, and by the following Thursday, we had *Live In Trouble* routined for its first performance. Barron had always made a point of recording the show each night on his portable cassette player, which proved to be invaluable to us not only at rehearsals, but also for keeping us on our toes during the performance. When we played back the recording of Thursday night's show, we couldn't believe the reaction; the laughter was so long and loud it covered other punchlines.

The entry in my diary on the 25th August read, 'The boys show no interest in playing or rehearsing the new record routine.'

I spent the following week securing parody clearances and booked the Beck Studios, Wellingborough, for the whole day of Friday 2nd September. These studios were run by the engineer/owner, Derek Tomkins who had the most wonderful Northamptonshire accent with a slow motion stutter! He had built the studio from scratch and we had already used it to make our cover albums, so we knew that the sounds were good and it was cheap!

The session had its ups and downs. Enthusiasm was running at a low ebb and for some the whole thing was a chore. We were booked to do a show in nearby Corby that night, so the others left at about 5 pm, while I stayed on to add a few more bits and attempt a mix. I had set myself an impossible task, as I had to be in Corby by 9 pm at the latest, so I eventually pleaded with Derek to let me come back after the show and work through the night. His answer was, 'I-I-I-I-I, d-d-d-don't mind a-a-at all.'

The next morning at 5 am, I left the studio with a couple of cassettes and the master tape under my arm, accompanied by a stinking headache. Derek chain-smoked, so the studio was like the funnel of the 'Queen Mary!' I slept until midday, but by

1 pm, I was back on the road heading north to Sheffield, where we had agreed to perform at an outdoor, fund-raising show for Radio Hallam; Beverley Chubb, the head of programming, had become a good friend of ours.

Within seconds of getting into the car, I played the cassette of *Live In Trouble*. I'd heard it a thousand times in the last twenty-four hours and I was convinced we had a big hit on our hands, but when the music had faded, there was a short silence before they unanimously agreed that they couldn't hear the words clearly enough. I blamed the player, the tyre noise and anything else I could think of to prove them wrong. Then I played it again. I was beginning to believe they could be right.

As soon as we reached Sheffield, I grabbed Beverley, sat her in the car and told her to listen carefully. She laughed a lot and as it came to an end, she said, 'If you remix it, you'll have a hit.'

What she was really saying was that she couldn't hear some of the words! As I'd already spent £175 at Beck Studios and knew how the boys felt about studio expenses, I couldn't ask for another day in the studio to do the remix.

My next task was to hawk *Live In Trouble* around the record companies. Tony, who would walk into any agency in London, refused to pass through the door of any record company. He didn't like that world of flash A&R departments but preferred to mix with the shady agents in Soho!

I had made three appointments for Tuesday, 6th September: at EMI, Pye and my first one with Lem Lubin at CBS in Soho Square. Lem, ex-bass player with Unit Four Plus Two, had left the road to become part of the A&R team at CBS and had given me his card when he'd come to see one of our shows. I didn't believe for one moment that I would ever be using it to try and secure a recording contract for the Barron Knights . . . neither did he.

After he had laughed a lot, Lem told me that CBS were in no

way a comedy label. However, I left the tape with him and asked him to play it to Dan Loggins, who was the head of A&R at that time. I'd return at 3 pm for an answer.

I felt reluctant about visiting EMI because they had refused to renew our contract back in 1971. We had now become established in the cabaret world and certainly were not the flavour of the month with them. Although Paul Watts sat and laughed at every line, I felt he was about to give me the same response as CBS. But this time my thoughts were way out of line. Paul offered a deal, providing we re-recorded it. He wasn't too happy with some of the sounds. (What did he expect for £175, Sergeant Pepper?) On the outside I was cool, but inside I was jumping about like a pogo stick. Here I was at EMI, Manchester Square, being offered a record deal. As I walked out of that large block of offices, feeling like a pools winner, I was 100% certain that we were heading for the charts.

From Manchester Square, I walked up to Cumberland Place to seek out Bob Page at Pye. He sat in his chair and listened, sniggered a couple of times, then called in a couple of the young secretaries for their opinion. Having watched their reaction to the song he knew it was something worth having. As with EMI, he suggested we should re-record at Pye, but with an in-house producer to oversee the session. I gave him the impression that we could agree on that, providing the deal included a big promotion with an album and another couple of singles.

A cab then took me to Berners Street, where I ran up three flights of stairs to my publisher's office. At the time I had no official deal with Warner Brothers Music, but between them the terrible twins Pete Reichardt and Rob Dickens gave me all the help I needed. It was Pete that had put me in touch with Paul Watts and Bob Page, so I was eager to tell him the good news. He was as pleased as punch, so he, Rob and I went to our regular watering hole, 'Annimos', a mad Greek restaurant in

Charlotte Street that was supported by the record industry. I always seemed to walk out of there feeling happy, but on that particular day, I felt like dancing on the tables and picking up the tab!

By 3 pm, I was back in Lem's office and, with two major labels bidding and a bottle of Greek wine in my blood system, I was not too bothered whether the answer was yea or nay.

'Dan likes the track and he wants to see you right away.'

Lem led me to Danny's office. I'd never met this tall, dark stranger before and with a hand as big as a dinner plate, he almost shook my wrist off its hinges! He had a real Californian drawl, 'Hey Peedder, I just love the track, it really cuts me up.' (Thinks . . . but we want to re-record it!)

'It has such a good feel about it. What sort of deal are you looking for?' I wasn't prepared for such a question, so I just replied, 'The best.'

Although he was prepared to take it as it stood, he wanted to alter the order of the parodies, which was easy to do with a sharp razor.

I left Danny and Lem and dashed back to Pete's office, to seek advice regarding a deal. He found it hard to believe that CBS would take on the Barron Knights and I found it hard to believe that I'd had offers from all three big boys. I rang Tony Avern from the Warner office and relayed the results of my day's work. By the time I arrived back in Leighton Buzzard, the boys agreed with me in thinking that CBS seemed the best bet and they were all very pleased with the outcome.

The following day Tony, for the first time in seven years, stepped inside a record company's front door. An hour later he came out again with a contract guaranteeing us £50,000, in return for three singles and an album each year for five years. The CBS promotion team were getting geared up to give the record a big push and it was a wonderful feeling, knowing that we were going to be high-profile once again. Within days, we were having a photo session at CBS in their basement studio and we also met all the 'pluggers', including Judd Lander and Roger Bowman. Simon Bates' wife Caroline was also there to assist if and when it became necessary: and it did, many times.

When *Live In Trouble* was released on 7th October, the initial reaction from Radio One was not too good, but many of the local radio stations gave it a push. Roger Finnigan on Piccadilly, Manchester, was particularly generous with his needle time. Judd Lander was in touch with us every day saying that we shouldn't leave the house because a certain radio station wanted us to take part in a phone-in. The major plugs were few and far between, so sales were slow, but we were assured that all was going to plan and to just sit tight.

Our first Radio One plug was by David Hamilton on Friday 21st and on the Saturday, Roger Pusey, 'Junior Choice' producer, allowed 'Stewpot' to give it a spin. Things were beginning to hot up!

The following Friday, when we had sold 55,000 copies, had made number 42 in the National charts and 27 in the Radio Luxembourg lists, we really felt that it was all about to happen. On 30th October, we opened at Caesars and the week broke all attendance records and hasn't been beaten yet!

We were all in a daze for most of the time, mainly because of our hectic schedule. Monday, Tuesday and Thursday, we were in De Lane Lee Studios, Wembley, recording tracks for an album, on Wednesday we recorded 'Top of the Pops' and on Friday we recorded the 'Tom O'Connor TV Special'.

Going on stage at 11 pm was tough, but the Caesars' audience were so good to us that it was almost like performing for your mates, and George Savva, the club manager, was having trouble coping with the number of people who wanted to see the show. If there was an old box lying around, he would lay a table cloth on it and sit half a dozen customers around it. I had never seen so many people in one room! The real hard work began after the show, when, with the sweat still pouring out, we used to go to the foyer and sign all the albums as they were sold. That personal touch doubled the sales and we would sell 200 units a night, not leaving until the last person had gone home. To this day we still sell albums and meet our fans after the show.

By the 14th November, our record had reached No. 14 in the charts and had sold more than 150,000 copies. We opened at the club in Charnock Richard, near Preston, and were glad of a good night's rest. On the Thursday, we flew from Manchester to London and back for another 'Top of the Pops', wondering how we were going to cope with another show. That night we were greeted in the dressing room by Les Dawson, who said, 'Don't be on too long, at these prices I can only afford one drink!'

As the compère announced us, we were yawning, but as soon as the spotlight hit us, we knew we were in for a good time. We had the audience in the palms of our hands and when they stood for an encore, we obliged. Les came into the dressing room with his drink and politely enquired, 'Excuse me lads, do you mind if I give you some constructive criticism?'

'Not a bit,' we all returned.

'Your act's crap!' He burst out laughing, put his arm around Butch and told him he was one of the funniest men in show biz (too true). We all collapsed in a heap, signed the albums and drank with Les until 4 am.

Radio One had played *Live In Trouble* a few more times, but not as many as we deserved, considering we had passed the quarter of a million sales mark. Disc jockeys seemed afraid of losing their credibility by playing a record by a group that took the rise out of the serious pop artistes. Regardless of the lack of air time, we were beginning to become very high-profile and had interviews with Jimmy Savile on 'Speakeasy', all the local TV stations, and as well as 'Top of the Pops', we appeared on 'Tiswas' three times in five weeks. To have Lenny Henry and Chris Tarrant bombard us with buckets of water was an easy way to reach the nation's record buyers. Whenever I told my friends that we were off to the 'Tiswas' studios, they pleaded for the chance to be locked up in the cage. I think Sally James might have had a part to play in their request.

The highest chart position achieved by *Live In Trouble* was No. 5 in Melody Maker but No. 7 in the NME and I was the happiest person in the world, as were the rest of the boys. Our last week of cabaret in 1977 was at the 'Circus Tavern', Purfleet, where on the Friday night, Maurice Oberstein, Judd Lander and a small party from CBS came to present us with a silver disc for the quarter million sales. The future looked wonderful and we as a unit, at last, couldn't wait to get back into the recording studio.

Six days before Christmas, we entered CBS Studios, Whitfield Street, to record our follow-up, *Back In Trouble Again*. It contained two of the most outstanding parodies we have ever written: new words to David Bowie's *Space Odyssey* and Queen's *Bohemian Rhapsody*. Getting permission for *Space Oddity* wasn't a problem, but it was quite a lucky break that secured the late Freddie Mercury's agreement. The hierarchy of CBS knew that Elton John was off to LA to meet up with Freddie, so Lem Lubin gave Elton a copy of our version, hoping for a favourable result. Apparently Freddie laughed at every word and, thank goodness, gave us his blessing. The third parody was of Meri Wilson's *Telephone Man*, which we changed to *Brewery Man*. Live on stage, they were the most powerful pieces we could ever wish for and we couldn't believe that they were all recorded on one side of our new single. We were pleased with the mix (at the time), and went home to enjoy Christmas, knowing for certain that we had another Top Ten hit in the can.

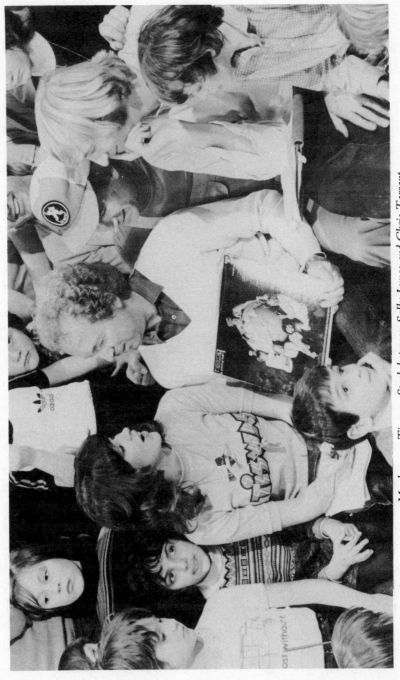

*Mayhem on Tiswas. Stuck between Sally James and Chris Tarrant.*

Not only did *Live In Trouble* revive the career of the Barron Knights, it gave everyone a different view of the future because, financially, we were secure for a few more years to come and everyone was more relaxed. There was one other important factor caused by our new-found fame and that was that every bit of humour produced twice the laughs. We didn't perform any differently, but audience reaction was so much stronger, to Butch in particular, which made him more relaxed in front of a crowd and consequently he gave himself more time to develop that wonderful sense of humour, which remains unique in our business.

1977 was definitely our come-back year. Having established ourselves with our Sixties hits and with all the experience of live performances behind us, it was a wonderful feeling to be back in the charts and to be given a 'second wind'. We had come to terms with our Image and the future looked fantastic. Christmas was a bit special that year

# *1978*

Our office in Leighton Buzzard was going crazy. Every theatre and club in the country wanted to book the Barron Knights. Our fee doubled, and in some cases trebled, but Tony always made sure that everyone concerned made money. He was a big believer in the long-term, repeat booking system. A club or theatre manager will look at his profit sheet first and at which act made that profit second and they will be the ones to get another booking.

We worked on New Year's Eve at the Royal Bath Hotel in Bournemouth, but I requested 2nd and 3rd January to be left free, because of a small operation that I was about to have . . . the big V!

I was going to have a vasectomy at a private clinic in Aylesbury, in fact it was the surgeon's private house. As I was walking towards his front door, I noticed a couple of teenage girls looking out a bedroom window; obviously his daughters, probably saying, 'There goes another one for the chop!' However, I was too concerned about my own well-being to worry about what they were thinking. My 9 am appointment was over within the hour and I drove back home without any pain. Veronica was so amazed that I was home early, that she doubted my bravery and swore I must have U-turned halfway to Aylesbury.

Early that afternoon, I began to ache, so I sat down in the lounge and relaxed in front of the TV. Within seconds, Flopsy our big fat cat decided to join me, so he leaped from the floor on to my lap. I screamed in agony and realized that the anaesthetic was beginning to wear off. My best pal John Williams and his wife Bernie were taking us out to dinner that evening, but we scrubbed that idea and ended up having a takeaway in front of the fire. I felt as if Red Rum himself had given me a good kick, somewhere between the knees and my belly button.

I'm sure Veronica must have a warped sense of humour. Two days later she insisted upon taking me to London, as there was a new film she wanted to see before it toured the provinces. I was still slightly sore but game for anything, as usual. She headed straight for Leicester Square and the new erotic film that was making headlines, *Emmanuelle*. I asked her why she wanted to see this load of garbage, as her taste in films doesn't usually sink to such depths.

'I want to make sure it still works,' she told me, with an

impish grin. Five days later, I reported back to the surgeon to check the success of his needlework. If ever I had wanted to film a moment in my life, it had to be the following five minutes; the scene would have won awards. As requested, I dropped my trousers to the floor. He undid the bandages and proceeded to inspect his work, then turned around and began to move things around on his desk. I was expecting him to tell me to pull up my trousers because all was well, but not a chance! He thrust an autograph book in my hand and asked me to sign it for his daughters. So there I was, pen and book in hand, willy looking decidedly unwell and asking, 'Who's it to?' The whole week was such a hoot that it inspired me to write a song, *The Big V*. We recorded it and gave it space on the *Knight Gallery* album.

> Is this your real wife?
> She's very fat you see,
> Look at her corsets
> Cos they're filled to capacity

Those were the opening lines to our parody of *Bohemian Rhapsody*. © 1974 EMI Music Publishing Limited.

When *Back In Trouble Again* was released on the 3rd February, Judd Lander rang with some news that we really didn't want to hear, Radio One refused to play it. We were dumbstruck. We had released a new record that was a better sound and was twice as funny as *Live In Trouble*, but the BBC would not play it to the nation. Doreen Davis was then Head of Radio One, and as we had known her for a very long time, I rang her to find out why we couldn't get our record played.

'Peter,' she said, 'you know I'm a big fan of the Barron Knights, but these lyrics are too rude. We have young children listening to Radio One and "Birth Control To Ginger Tom" is just too vulgar for us and besides, fat people might be offended at your new "Queen" lyrics.'

To say that we were upset was an understatement.

Play the Sex Pistols, they're good fun: but don't play the Barron Knights' record, it's offensive!

'You will never beat the system,' were the famous last words from Judd. He insisted that no matter how hard we tried, Doreen would not change her mind and the only alternative we had was to forget it and come up with an idea for a song of which the Beeb would approve. In the past, the thought that anything we wrote could be offensive to anyone hadn't crossed our minds, but now every line that we wrote was scrutinised, just in case.

With *Back In Trouble Again* tucked away in the bottom drawer, never to be heard again, the 'writing machine' was well and truly in motion again. It was wonderful to see Butch and Barron inspired with such good ideas.

One teatime, I sat down and watched 'Blue Peter' and saw John Noakes in the garden with the country's favourite gardener, Percy Thrower. John had a problem trying to control his dog Shep and he kept saying, 'Get down, Shep.' I found it so amusing that I went into my studio the same night and wrote a song about John and his dog and called it *Get Down Shep*. It took me about ten minutes and when I played my simple little demo to my family and friends they all instantly associated with the idea. I had a little hunch I had the beginnings of a national catch-phrase!

On Sunday, 11th June, the Barron Knights and their wives were invited by ELO to their concert at Wembley. It was a most spectacular show, which began with a flying saucer rising from the stage: then the undercarriage opened up to reveal their light show. We were sitting six rows from the front and speakers were aimed at us from all directions. The sound almost blew our brains out! At the end of the show, Jeff Lynne and Kelly Groucutt invited us backstage for a chat, but my ears were still ringing and I didn't hear a word.

*Fathers and sons.*

So, to go from the sublime to the 'gor blimey', the next day we were back at Wembley in De Lane Lee Studio 4, to record *Get Down Shep*. It was hard not to feel envious; ELO had, quite deservedly, filled a seven thousand seater stadium, while silly us merely had *Get Down Shep* to contend with! However, the track was finished and mixed by lunchtime and so in the afternoon, we recorded a spoof of the Gladys Knight song *The Way We Were*; a story about remembering all the things that were around when we were kids, like ration books and farthings.

We opened at Watford Bailey's on Sunday, 25th June and the show on the Wednesday was in aid of 'Save the Children', in the presence of Her Royal Highness, Princess Anne. We had the great honour of meeting her before the show, but to see her laugh at our jokes and songs made the night even more special.

Russell Harty was sitting next to the Princess that evening, and after the performance he invited us to the table. At that time, his TV chat show was the one to be seen on and within the time it took to down a glass of warm Watford wine, we had been asked to appear the very next night. We took along our 'Sons of Barron Knights', the look-alike dummies that were part of our live show for years, and we also sang our *Space Oddity* parody and did ourselves a lot of good.

The week ended on a high spot for me. ATS, the tyre company, sponsor one of the biggest pro-am tournaments on the golf calendar, which was held at my home course, Woburn Golf and Country Club. I was drawn with the Spaniard, Manuel Pinero and was having a good day; my driving was straight and the putts were dropping! Coming down the eighteenth fairway, we were told that we needed a birdie to win. There were two teams behind us that had no chance, so the knuckles went white! I hit a seven iron to within 6 ft of the hole and Manuel hit a nine iron 8 ft away and then, he missed his putt. A thousand people watched me line up my putt and my knees shook as I hit the ball . . . into the hole.

We were backwards and forwards to De Lane Lee Studios putting together material for another album. Dick Lewzey and Dave Hunt, our engineers, had all the qualities needed to cope with one of our sessions. Engineers are a breed all on their own and seem to have both built-in stamina and incredible patience. We managed to complete *The Big V*, *My Will* and *Air On A G-String* before we all took a break to recharge our batteries.

Veronica, Tanya and I hired a villa in the Algarve, where we had hot sun and blue sky for two weeks. Apart from when I succumbed to a touch of food poisoning from the local sardines, I hardly rose from my sun lounger during the whole period. While watching Tanya having a swim, I noticed that her bikini bottom had slipped, revealing the line between her tan and her little white bum. My brain seemed to be permanently locked into writing those parodies, so what else could this be but a cue for new words to sing to *Little White Bull*?

144

'Once upon a time I had a little white bum . . .' That was it. I spent two days of the holiday writing the whole thing and at a later stage we improved it, recorded it and the song became part of our act for ten years.

We started live work again on the 3rd September at the 'Talk of the South', St Agnes, on the North Cornwall coast. Obviously, we had all benefited from the holiday as I can't remember a week when we were more productive. Ideas were pouring out. Our support act was Zoe Black, a Liverpool singer, who made a funny remark about every five seconds and helped to keep us all in the right mood for writing comedy. *Boogie Nights* became *Boozy Nights* and we completed a parody of *The Three Bells* based on a story told by Tony Silvey, a local rugby star and mate of Duke, about pinching lead from the chapel roof. By the end of the week we had not only completed the writing, but Butch had worked out the harmonies, ready for a live debut! It's been the longest serving song in our up and down and up again career.

When Dan Loggins left CBS London to become the head of A&R in New York, he was replaced by Muff Winwood and his assistant, Nicky Graham. We were in the process of completing a medley that we were sure would meet with BBC approval, when, to our surprise, Muff suggested that we make *Get Down Shep* our next single. Once again, the 'big guns' of Radio One refused to give it air time, but Stewpot played it one Saturday morning and from then on it was regularly requested. Although it sold only twenty thousand copies, it became the most played Barron Knights record. Many years later in 1992, while we were being interviewed by Simon Groom on BBC Radio Bedfordshire, we offered two free tickets for a local concert in Bedford to the person who could answer the following question, 'What was the Barron Knights' biggest hit?'

145

The first thirty 'phone callers all said *Get Down Shep*. We've had fourteen hits, some selling over half a million, yet most people thought that *Get Down Shep* was our biggest success. It proves the Bruce Forsyth theory, that a catch-phrase is forever! I will treasure my 'Get Down Shep' badge for the rest of my life, unless the 'Hard Rock Café' offers me 'megabucks' to hang it on their wall.

The record reached number 52 and Christmas was approaching, so Muff wanted to catch the seasonal market and re-release it! I went 'spare'! *Taste Of Aggro* was the best thing we had ever done, a possible million-seller, yet it was still sitting on his desk, waiting to hit the British people.

# *Taste of Aggro*

We were always in a hurry when we made records. If a session started at 10 am, hopefully we would be recording within fifteen minutes. Dave and Dick at De Lane Lee Studios never could get used to the speed at which we wanted things done, although I would always ring the studio the day before, to let them know of our requirements.

*Taste Of Aggro* was recorded in seven hours on the 19th September. The medley was based on such originals as, *Rivers Of Babylon*, *The Smurf Song* and *Matchstalk Men And Matchstalk Cats And Dogs*. We decided, this time, not to include the sound of audience laughter and applause, because Dave Lee Travis had made a comment about it spoiling *Live In Trouble*. We all took cassettes of the recording home with us and all came to the same conclusion; it lacked the atmosphere of our past records, but all that was missing was the audience reactions. We had to ignore DLT and do what we believed was right.

We persuaded Muff not to re-release *Get Down Shep*, which caused instant panic at CBS, who wanted the master tape of *Taste Of Aggro* instantly. I took the multi-track tape with me to Manchester, where we were performing four shows at the 'Willows' in Salford and we stole a couple of days studio time at 'Arrow Sound' and added the laughter and applause to the recording. In some spare time, we recorded a comedy version of *Air On A G-String*. We were pleased with the results of both recordings.

The album, including *Taste Of Aggro* was delivered to Muff on the 5th October, the Barron Knights' 18th Birthday. We were all very proud of the standard of writing and knew that with the correct marketing it could become a classic comedy album. *Boozy Nights*, *Little White Bum*, *Chapel Lead Is Missing*, *Get Down Shep*, *Big V* and several more, were aimed at a certain market that had been starved of comedy on record since the days of Spike Jones.

Both the single and the album were released on 17th November and the response from the Radio One team was overwhelming. Paul Burnett had a 'Fun at One' spot and he made it his record of the week: we also won the public's pop panel vote on the Tony Blackburn Show, which meant he had to play it every day (much against his will), and if that wasn't enough, Noel Edmonds featured our *Knight Gallery* album on his Sunday morning show.

It has never been easy to market the Barron Knights on disc. Our act is classified as 'Novelty', an area usually reserved for the one-off single by an artiste who is never heard of on record, ever again. We wanted to continue to build up a following that would always buy our albums and singles. It was the

*Presentation of our first gold album by Pete Reichardt, 2nd left and Rob Dickens, 3rd right.*

most difficult task and although we gave CBS a good product, they needed every bit of publicity and every plug that was available to an artiste.

Apart from all the Radio One support, we had a 'Pebble Mill' TV spot and the Saturday morning 'Banana TV' in Southampton. It was saturation at its best and the result was predictable. We entered the charts at No. 19! In the first week we sold 150,000 copies and our daily sales were even outstripping *Do Ya Think I'm Sexy*, the song that Rod Stewart had taken to the number one slot. 'Top of the Pops' went to the trouble of making a quick video and after that was broadcast, the sales doubled. Maurice Oberstein invited us into his top floor office at CBS for a champagne reception on Tuesday, the 5th December to announce that we had broken Abba's daily sales record figure! 60,000 copies sold in one day was a lot of records and we just couldn't believe it. The following day, I went into the sales office and watched the computer notch up an incredible 62,000! We jumped to number 4 and the whole record business was backing either us or Boney M for the Christmas number one position. We finally stuck at number three. With sales of 960,000, were we bothered? Of course we bloody were!

Selling a million units would have been too much to ask, but if we had, we couldn't have asked for a better finish to the year. I was in seventh heaven and I felt so wonderful that I bought three airline tickets to Austria, and Veronica, Tanya and I spent two weeks skiing in the Tyrol.

# 1979 – Awards Year

Having had so much to celebrate that Christmas, we all met up again on the 14th January and that night we opened up at 'Blazers' in Windsor. Dear George Savva had moved from Caesars, in Luton to take charge there. Every night we played to a capacity audience, but on the Saturday, we gave poor George a fright. We flew to Amsterdam early in the morning for a TV show and were delayed by fog on our return trip, so we rang George to tell him it was possible that we could be a few minutes late. At 10 pm we landed at Heathrow, knowing that we were due on stage at 11 pm. It seemed as though we waited ages for the luggage, but we arrived outside the club with five minutes to spare. George was on the pavement, sweat on his upper lip, puffing away at a ciggy, and he said, 'Don't panic lads, you're not due on until ten past!'

On the 23rd January, this intrepid band of pretend pop stars found themselves in the middle of the desert between Dubai and Abu Dhabi performing to men only.

One of Butch's friends was boss of Dutco Pauling, a construction company whose employees had nothing to spend their money on except drink so they paid our air fares and a fee so that we could give them a show. From that one Arabian night, we have built up an annual tour of Middle Eastern cities. Bahrain, Muscat, Dubai and Abu Dhabi are regular destinations.

The El Ain Hilton was the setting for an outdoor concert. The demand for tickets was so great that their function room was quite inadequate, which resulted in us being given this wonderfully exotic, open air setting for the show, until, for the first time in two years . . . it rained! With the help of their mainly Philippino staff, the equipment was transferred to the ballroom and we sat the crowd on the floor and anywhere else they could park their bums!

The Middle East has become a very good part of the world for shows and I'm led to believe that we were the pioneers! The venues are, as a rule, the big hotels that have been built to the standard of a Sheikh's palace. The entrances to these hotels are very grand and somewhere in a corner will be an Arab, cross-legged on his expensive carpet, offering an egg-cup full of black coffee from his brass pot and a puff of something wonderful! This is, a traditional symbol of Arabian hospitality, originating from the days when they lived in tents. On my first visit, I was dumbfounded at the number of Arab men who walk together holding hands. They also resent anyone staring at their ladies. At Dubai airport, I watched three women, all dressed in black with their faces hidden, say goodbye to someone who I presumed was their husband and father. After they'd been through passport control, the three began chatting away to one another as though they'd never talked before and as soon as the aircraft took off, they removed their masks and laughed and giggled all the way to Muscat. It is absolutely amazing that these women are prepared to put up with wearing something that must be so uncomfortable and is the ugliest article of clothing ever to have been designed.

They call the Emirates Golf Club in Dubai the eighth wonder of the world. After a half-hour drive into the desert, suddenly you come across the wondrous sight of three white buildings that have been designed to look like a Bedouin camp: this is the Club House! It has a giant swimming pool where if you want a drink, you just swim to the middle, while a million gallons of water a day keep the course permanently green. Carol Read, who is the PR for the whole complex, came to see our show and very kindly invited me to play the course. I was down to play with two lady members, so I thought I was in for a pleasant day, but at the last minute, I was taken to the bar and introduced to Prince Kais Bin Tarik Al Said, who is a cousin of the Sultan of Oman.

After a very formal introduction, he asked me my profession and on hearing the name Barron Knights, his little dark face lit up with a very friendly smile. Not only had he seen the act many times, but his secretary was a Kiwi girl who came to England with Barron's future second wife. I asked him where he had seen the show, expecting him to say the Palladium or Talk of the Town, but where did he see us? The Playhouse Theatre, Weston-super-Mare! After a couple of drinks, he called me Pete, I called him 'Treasure' and away we went to play a very pleasant round of golf.

We are often asked about our audiences in the Middle East. We always perform at a dinner cabaret which is attended by doctors, nurses, airline pilots, accountants and the executives of the construction and oil industries. They are mainly English and have plenty of fun out there in the desert, where there is not too much to spend your money on except food and drink, and there are plenty of both. Most men are able to have their wives and family with them and they all look extremely tanned, but would give anything to have the opportunity to walk in the pouring rain!

We ended the month with a week at the 'Golden Garter', Manchester, where on the opening night, in the middle of Duke's ballad, Judd Lander walked on stage and presented us with a gold album for a million pounds worth of sales, and a gold single for the same reason.

On the 18th March, we were at Blazers, Windsor again, this time receiving the Club Mirror Award for 'Best Act', but even that was overshadowed by the news that Tony relayed to us in the dressing room, five minutes before we were due on stage.

As he poured us each a glass of champagne, he announced that we had won the 'Nationwide Golden Award'. This was part of the British Rock and Pop Awards and decided by votes from the British public. The category we had won was 'Most Popular British Entertainers' and was set up by the BBC Nationwide programme. It's probably our most satisfying award to date.

Presentation day was 11th April and it certainly was a day of emotions. The BBC had arranged for two Rolls Royces to collect us and our wives from our homes and deliver the happy bunch to the Cafe Royal in Regent Street, where we met our fellow award winners: the Bee Gees, Gerry Rafferty, ELO, Leo Sayer and Ian Dury. The event was televised and our profile reached an all-time high.

We were unable to celebrate with our wives that night because of an engagement at the Wakefield Theatre Club, however we drank a few bottles of champagne between Kings Cross and Wakefield station, and when we arrived in the dressing room, there we found a big box, beautifully wrapped, but we all stood back waiting for someone to open this big surprise. (Were we being polite, or were we just pissed?) However, after our 'staggering' performance, we finally managed to rip open 'Pandora's box' and, oh dear, it was another dozen bottles of Moet Chandon, sent with the Manager's compliments, plus an invitation to a party at his home on the outskirts of town!

We arrived at this magnificent house about 1 am, when the party was in full swing, with exotic food and champagne being trodden into the expensive carpets; but no one seemed to notice, they were having so much fun. At one point, I believe that the burglar alarm went off for about five minutes, but they just turned the music up louder to compensate!

At 5 am, taxis began to arrive to ferry us all home, although Butch, having his own car, had left much earlier. I really didn't feel very well, which wasn't surprising after spending most of the day and night drinking. Getting up at 8 am to play golf with my good Yorkshire friend, Tony Richardson was the last thing I fancied, but I couldn't let Tony down. I arranged for an alarm call and I still did not feel at all well when this young female voice announced it was time for me to rise and that Tony was waiting for me in reception. I performed a technicolour yawn in the toilet and had to stop four times before we reached Selby Golf Club, where I also left a few fairway 'pizzas' lying around.

They say that success breeds success, but in this case it definitely gave rise to an inability to cope!

The awards were something that we never expected to receive, but they mean a lot to us as a reminder and a token of recognition of the fun we have given the British public. (We were also rewarded for the best musical advert when one of the three Smarties adverts written by us, got the vote at the Cannes Festival.)

Throughout the summer of '79, we worked very hard on creating material for the new album, including songs about David Bellamy, Mork and Mindy and a parody of *Macarthur Park* written by my brother; it was a story about a gardener, called Arthur Clark.

The album was called *Teach The World To Laugh* and contained two tracks that made quite an impact, but in totally different ways.

The *Logical Song* had been a big hit for Supertramp in the States and Dave's brother-in-law had written a parody of it appertaining to the gas crisis. We recorded two versions, one with his lyrics and the other slightly adapted for the British market, but both were called *Topical Song*. Our recording of *Boozy Nights* had failed, disappointingly, as a single, so we quickly followed it with the *Topical Song* with which we had no success either. One day, when we were having our album sleeve photo taken, Judd rang to tell us that the American

154

version had entered 'Billboard' charts at No. 42; hence the big grins in the picture on the front of the sleeve! I never thought I'd live to see the day when the Barron Knights would be in the American charts, even if it was for only a couple of weeks.

Then Barron wrote a story about a poor guy waiting on the tarmac at Heathrow. It was a parody of John Denver's *Leaving On A Jet Plane* and a great idea, but somehow lacked spice, so I suggested it was changed to *Heaving On A Jet Plane*. This really opened the flood gates for funny lyrics! The publishers, suprisingly, gave us permission to use it and the routine has served us well all around the world. It's still in the act after thirteen years, but not without having had its share of controversy.

Whenever we tour Australia, it has become routine for us to visit every local radio station to have a chat and promote the show and, more often than not, the DJ will choose to play *Heaving On A Jet Plane* which seems to be an Aussie favourite, mainly due to the fact that it's about a 'chunder'.

John Denver just happened to be touring the country at the same time and was also in and out of the radio stations. When he was asked by a certain DJ what he thought of our version of his classic, he knew nothing about it: so the DJ played it to him and J. D. went crazy! He rang Essex Music in London and threatened to take his business away from them, unless the agreement with us was cancelled. We had no idea at the time of what was going on. On our return from Oz, we began filming a one-hour Special for Channel 4, which involved renting a Brittania-owned 727 at Luton Airport to film scenes for *Heaving On A Jet Plane*.

Three days later, we were told by Essex Music to scrap the whole idea.

Our agency, 'Templar Entertainments', started to get really busy so Tony employed Doug Olney to handle the smaller, time-consuming jobs. Yvonne Busby had been our loyal secretary for many years and how she managed to work in the thick smoke that constantly surrounded her will always remain a mystery.

One of the acts that Tony found work for were the 'Zodiacs', a husband and wife team that specialised in mind reading. She would stand blindfolded on stage and with her back to the audience, while he walked among the audience, picked up an object and asked her a question.

'Take your TIME, what is it I am holding in my left hand'?

'A watch,' she would say in a most dramatic way.

'SEE if you can guess what I'm holding.'

'Is it a pair of Glasses? ! ! ! !'

'Isn't that amazing, ladies and gentlemen?'

One morning Tony had a phone call from Mr Zodiac.

'Hello Tony, regarding the job in Worthing, how much are we getting?' Tony's reply was, 'You're the bloody mind reader!' and he slammed the phone down.

Nicky White was a magician who had a bad stammer.

'T-T-T-T-T-Tony, w-w-w-what t-t-t-time i-i-i-is the s-s-s-show i-i-i-in D-D-D-Dag-Dag- Dag . . .'

The impatient Tony said, 'If you're coming, cough'.

At one time, an agent offered £3000 for the Barron Knights to perform on a Tuesday night and Tony told him that we wouldn't work it because it was the night that 'Ironside' was on the TV!

21a Bridge Street, Leighton Buzzard, was our office for fifteen years and Tony's daily tasks began with climbing two flights of narrow stairs which led to the dingy, tatty rooms. He never wanted to work in luxurious surroundings; he saw enough of that in the London offices of the big agents and knew who was paying for the upkeep.

1979 ended with the release of *Food For Thought*, another

parody medley that reached a disappointing chart position of 46, although the album did slightly better, selling 50,000 units. On reflection it would have been almost impossible to better 1978, but we gave it all we could at the time.

As Christmas approached, we appeared on two consecutive editions of the programme 'Tiswas' and in one of them we were asked to do a song which had connections with getting wet! We sang *Cool Water* and the result was the funniest three minutes in our television history. As we sang, Chris Tarrant and Lenny Henry cruelly slung large buckets of water straight into our faces; the resulting camera close-ups were brilliant and the timing could never have been rehearsed. We tried to repeat the scene on our Channel 4 Special, but it was impossible to recreate. 'Tiswas' was our last show of the year.

# 1980

We wanted to have a crack at America as it seemed a natural progression in our career and we'd had a small success in the charts there a few months earlier. So, Butch and I went on a mission to find out how to make them laugh.

We arrived in New York on 2nd January and found that it was fifteen degrees below freezing, so they got the first laugh! Although we had made an arrangement to see Jonathan King on our arrival, we were so tired as a result of the journey (and a bottle of full-bodied Burgundy), that we gave it a miss until the following day.

Around mid-morning we arrived at his flat to find him

almost buried in newspapers that were piled four feet high and covering every square inch of floor space. Having made us coffee and talked about himself for a couple of hours, he then proclaimed that it was going to be tough for us, but we'd done the right thing in coming to visit!

It snowed heavily that night as we ran from our hotel in the Avenue of Americas to a Bistro on the opposite side of the road and the temperature had dropped to 20 degrees below!

After a couple of days in the Big Frozen Apple, we flew to Nashville, where we stayed at the Spence Manor Hotel, recommended to us by Pete Reichardt. While Butch was waiting to collect our luggage, I found a Spence Manor 'phone and asked for the hotel car to collect us. Twenty minutes later, a black stretch limo pulled up, out jumped the driver and as he combed his Elvis style hair, he said to us in his Tennessee drawl, 'Mr Bakerrr and Mr Langforrrd, ahm fram the Spaynce Manorrr Howtell, welcome ta Nayshvielle.'

While he put the luggage into the 'trunk', we got lost amongst the back seat! It was exactly as we'd seen in the films: a television, champagne, enough leg room for the Harlem Globe Trotters and tinted glass, so we wouldn't be recognised in Nashville High Street!

'What are we doing here?' Butch said, as he sat with his legs out straight in a car for the first time in his life. When we arrived at the hotel, we searched for a coffee shop, but to no avail. It seemed that anything you wanted was delivered to your room.

We couldn't wait to explore this musically historic town and our first stop was across the road at Conway Twitty's Music City (which was just like 'Sainsburys' but sold only records and cassettes), where I bought anything by Ray Stevens that was missing from my collection back home.

Next, we saw Tim Whipperman at Warner Brothers Publishers, who was most helpful with a few ideas and suggested that we went to the Exit Inn, to see the real country music. Our driver, 'Elvis', took us right to the door and for the next few hours we sat absolutely mesmerised at what was around us. The group on stage gave a fairly mediocre performance, and yet the crowd stood up after every song and yelled things like 'Whoopee', 'Yippie' and 'alright'. I think they were all stoned! After a while, we were warned that there could be a possible 'shoot out', so we rang for 'Elvis', who came and picked up his mates from Leighton Buzzard.

Once the prolific writing team of Roger Cooke and Roger Greenaway had gone their separate ways, Mr Cooke had moved to Nashville. We'd been exchanging letters for a couple of years, so it was fun to meet up with him on the last day, when he and his partner, Ralph Murphy, inspired us to hope that there was room for the Barron Knights' style of humour in the 'Country' market. After a few lunchtime Chardonnays, Roger and Ralph decided they would run us to the airport at Nigel Mansell speed through a heavy rain storm. Not only had they drunk a few too many beers, but they had been smoking the 'funny' stuff and in those circumstances, the last thing we needed was to be delayed. But, sure enough, we were and that was the excuse to head for the bar. Butch and I eventually flew to Los Angeles via Memphis: but we don't remember much about Memphis!

The temperature in Los Angeles was 80 degrees, not bad for the first week of January. We made our way to Warner Publishing on Sunset Boulevard, where professional manager Mike Sandovil, knowing of our success back in the UK, gave us a few ideas. He also gave us guitars, studio time, a room with bare walls and a piano with which Butch recorded a new version of *Space Invaders*, assisted by the in-house engineer, while I wrote a song about the San Andreas fault. By early evening, we were both exhausted but Mike had invited us to go to Marine del Ray to see Ricky Lee Jones. Butch took a 'rain check', but I went along out of interest and she was great, but I was too zonked out to enjoy it.

We couldn't leave LA without saying hello to my very first publisher, Cyril Shane. He had retired to the San Fernando Valley, but could still quote titles that I had forgotten, or thought I had!

We arrived back in London on 13th January, knowing we could make our mark in the States, but it would have to be a long term commitment and at the moment, there was too much at stake in the UK for us to leave and give it a go.

The next few months were spent working the usual round of clubs and writing a new album. Thankfully, we were never short of ideas, it was just coming up with a commercially viable one that was the problem.

The last day of May saw us flying on Air Florida to Miami, where Michael Black, the most charasmatic agent that our business has ever known, had booked us to perform for two weeks at the Newport Beach Hotel on Collins Avenue.

The Americans are the best at promotion and marketing and they had certainly filled every hour of the day for us. On our first morning there, they stuck us on the top of an open double decker bus, as it was driven around the streets with loud speakers blaring out one of Butch's compositions for the new album, *Oh Miami*. The result was that in the afternoon, every newspaper reporter wanted an angle for a story and later in the evening, we were interviewed on the radio chat show hosted by Alan Burk, the only DJ to work with a loaded gun on his desk. We left the studio in quite a nervous state, stupidly got lost and found ourselves in the middle of a 'no go' black area. We were about to ask for directions when a cop car drew up.

'If you wanna stay alive get the f . . . out of here,' said the fat policeman from Dade County. We didn't like to tell him that we were from Leighton Buzzard and only wanted to know the way to the sea!

At last we arrived back at our hotel rooms and found we each had a memo slipped under the door, saying, 'Rehearsals will be at 11 am in the Ocean room' – signed 'Chuck Shlackman'. We woke up next morning to find another memo, 'There will be a photo call at 11.30 am, in the Ocean room' – signed 'Chuck Shlackman'. By the time I'd had a shower, yet another envelope had been slipped under the door.

'The Managing Director, Mr Freddie Rosani would like to extend to you an invitation to breakfast in the Bistro on the ground floor' – signed 'Chuck Shlackman'.

Our opening night in the 'Seven Seas' lounge was a big success and the critics were more than generous. Bill von Maurer of the Miami News wrote, 'The Barron Knights' comedy is delicious and once you catch the tempo of what they are doing, you want to hear more and more. If there is any complaint about the Knights' show, it is that they simply aren't on stage long enough. They should have more exposure to the Americans. There are 200 million of you, where are you? We owe it to the Barron Knights for their courage in being in the forefront of what is to be a new wave of British talent. They are original and give us Americans a refreshing break from humour that is too familiar. Nobody can beat the British when it comes to using a rapier instead of a bludgeon as an instrument of comic satire.'

Once 'Memo man' Chuck had used up a whole tree for his messages, we were able to relax and enjoy the weather. Michael Black and us pink-bodied lads were relaxing by the pool one day, when this very large lady pulled herself up the ladder and out of the water. It was like watching Moby Dick heaving himself onto dry land. Quick as a flash Michael, in his best Mill Hill Jewish accent said, 'Excuse me love, were there any other survivors?' He and I were holding onto the rail at the deep end, when he noticed four Jewish people talking under an umbrella on the opposite side of the pool. He had a bet with me that they would be talking about food.

'Old fat Jewish people only talk about food,' he spluttered. I swam the full length of the olympic size pool and held on to the rail so that I could listen to what they were saying.

'So we stood in line for twenty minutes, but boy was it worth it. We had T-bones that big and as much salad as you could eat.' Michael was right and I lost the bet.

Freddie Rosani invited us to the races and lo and behold, there in the programme, the third race was named 'The Barron Knights Stakes'. I lost twenty dollars!

When it was time to leave, Matt Munro's daughter, Michelle, gave us a drunken send-off when she invited us to her Dad's place about ten miles up the coast and put on a spread fit for the lady who had emerged from the pool!

It's sad that we haven't managed to have more exposure in the States. They don't have anything comparable now, which is strange when you think that we based our act on the Four Preps back in 1960. It has worked in Australia, South Africa and the Far East, so why not the USA?

We decided to call the next album *Jest A Giggle* and were well ahead of schedule, when we made a group decision to purpose-write a Christmas parody.

Butch had walked into the dressing room at the 'Circus Tavern', Purfleet raving over a TV show about dog training that he'd seen. In our show that night, when he raised his hand and said 'Sit', the audience howled with laughter, so the next time it appeared on TV, I was glued to the box like the rest of the country. Barbara Woodhouse was rapidly becoming a household name, so with my tiny brain echoing with memories of *Get Down Shep*, I decided I had to write a song about her and her training methods and call it *The Sit Song*.

When you have a subject as varied and topical as this was,

*With Barbara Woodhouse at her home in Hertfordshire. Note how she made Duke and Barron 'SIT'.*

everything becomes too easy; so within a couple of hours, the song was ready for the studio. We zipped along to Wapalong Studios in Luton and with the help of John Baccini, the engineer, we recorded a very tight backing track. After adding the vocals at De Lane Lee Studios, Wembley, suddenly we had a surprise single ready.

CBS were enthusiastic, so everything fell into place. It was a perfect song for the 'Stewpot' show, so he gave us a few plugs and after a Pebble Mill TV slot, it reached No. 44 in the National charts. When chat show host, Michael Parkinson, set up one of his famous interviews with Barbara Woodhouse, he also invited us along to sing the song and while I was performing it, the floor manager surprised me by letting loose a dog: a mechanical one, I hasten to add!

I call that style of writing my 'silly little songs', but in retrospect, they have served us well through the years. They are easy to perform, cheap to record and Oh, how I wish there were more ideas around to inspire me!

Following on from a minor hit was a great stepping stone for our Christmas offering *Never Mind The Presents*. Once again, we knew we would be bound to face fierce criticism from the DJ's, so we worked very hard on the lyrics and the result was a track with which we felt very happy. It was a great relief when we received permission for our new lyrics to *Brick In The Wall*:

> Christmas turkey you can stuff it
> Roast potatoes sprouts and all
> Who's this geezer Father Christmas?
> He's so stoned he's lost control.

The words we sang to the *Sparrow Song* were equally impressive:

> I'm only a poor little fairy
> They stuck me on top of this tree
> They switched on the lights

And bang went my tights
And my legs fell off one two three.

The video we made was extremely funny, with Barron dressed as Santa driving a motorbike through a ten foot brick wall and to see Butch dressed as a fairy was something I must remember to tell his mother about one day!

We reached No. 17 and therefore the festive season should have been a happy time for us all; but a certain tragedy tarnished those few weeks for us.

On the 9th December, Barron and I were in Norwich for an Anglia Television chat show and together with Scottish comedian, Billy Connelly, we were enjoying a good English Breakfast, when over the radio the newscaster announced that John Lennon had been shot dead! We sat there in disbelief as our thoughts went back to those wonderful three weeks we had spent with the Beatles. A man who had given the world so much pleasure, had been wiped out in seconds.

# *1981*

This was a problem year for me. When I decided to write this book, I spent about six months gathering all the information from my boxes of memorabilia, but a month of that time was spent searching for my 1981 diary. Unfortunately, I had to give it up as lost, so I wrote from photographs I had in an album of the same year.

★

Although CBS had performed wonders in other parts of the world, it was mainly in Australia that our albums had sold very well. So there was a demand for our show.

When Val Doonican was touring Oz, he had very kindly recommended us to his agent Tony Brady who, while he was staying in England, was introduced to Tony Avern and between them they set up a tour across the whole of Australia, which has now been a regular feature of our yearly plans ever since. The variety of show venues that Mr Brady sets up is, to say the least, unbelievable. On arrival in Sydney, we are asked to appear on a lunch time TV chat show; then we perform four or five live shows in Sydney, usually the League Clubs. After flying to Cairns in Queensland, we work the theatres all the way down the coast to Surfers' Paradise: Townsville, Mackay, Ayr, Rockhampton and Brisbane are the usual stops. A two-hour drive inland from Brisbane leads to the garden city of Toowoomba, where the audience is made up mainly of broccoli farmers.

A week at Tweed Heads gives us a rest from travelling and it is also the home of the biggest and best nightclub in Australia, 'Seagulls'. We lie on Coolangatta beach all day, perform the show at night and then have a nice drink before crashing out. It's our little treat to ourselves!

Two days in Melbourne, followed by two days in Adelaide bring us through to Perth and if ever a city was blessed with all things good, Perth was the chosen place. The Swan river meanders its way from Freemantle, past the city and out towards the vineyards. Sitting on a hill, Kings Park offers bush walks as well as beautiful flora and long stretches of lush lawns. If a six car tail-back occurs, it's reported on the radio and rush hour lasts a mere five minutes.

We performed to our biggest audience ever on the lawns between the river and the city. 40,000 people had come to see our 'Australia Day' concert, which was linked up with the FM radio station. The climax to the evening was to be a firework display, with the biggest rocket ever lighting up the sky: they named it the Chrysanthemum. The display was timed by computers to synchronise with the music from *War Of The Worlds*. The vast crowd had been 'ooing and aahing' for about twenty minutes, when suddenly, the whole of the city was lit up by this enormous spread of sparkling colour, twice the size of Wembley stadium. There was a big cheer, loud applause and the folks began to wander away, when, to their surprise, the display started up again, ending with a few crackers and tiny sprays. Not much of a finale, more like, dare I say, a bit of a damp squib!

In the paper the next day, it was revealed that a spark had caught the touch paper on the 'Chrysanthemum' and set it off prematurely. Bring back the box of matches and the man with the torch!

It was the first and only time we had worked to a crowd of that size. The staging was fifty metres square and the sound equipment was as big as a house! To watch a sea of people waving and dancing to our comedy songs was very funny and gave us a glimpse of what it must be like for Paul McCartney every time he steps on stage.

The following night, we performed at 'Ramanos', Perth's biggest night club which was filled to capacity with a crowd totalling two hundred and twenty!

If I were ever to consider leaving England, Perth would be my choice of somewhere else to live. I've seen most of the world and every place has its good and bad points, but this city in Western Australia is hard to criticise. It has all the good things I like about life; space, wonderful climate, beautiful countryside and many friends.

Guitar legend, Hank B Marvin, became a resident of Perth and lives in a beautiful mock Tudor house in the hills, overlooking the vineyards. On each of our visits to Australia, we make a point of meeting up with him, that is if we can drag him away from the garden or tennis court. As he's very handy with a fork and spade, we dare not visit without taking him a new shrub to plant. Veronica and I went through the process of purchasing a seven acre plot of land in the same Brigadoon Hills, but unfortunately, the Australian High Commission didn't think I was suitable material to become a new Australian.

While we were in Mackay, Queensland, we found ourselves with a day off, so Butch, Tony, Barron and I hopped onto a giant catamaran in search of Brampton Island, which is part of the Whitsunday Islands and about a mile square with white sandy beaches, palm trees and a crystal clear sea. Barron disappeared for an hour, while the rest of us snoozed on the beach in this idyllic setting, with the sea breeze keeping the air cool. He eventually returned with a canoe and paddle and insisted we all went for a ride. The canoe was built for only two at the most, but like fools we all climbed in and with a push from the beach, we were off, heading out to the open sea. We must have been about half a mile out, when we decided to head back to shore, but as we were turning, we noticed how fast the current was moving and the more we tried to turn, the harder it was to control the canoe. Quick as a flash, we toppled over and the four of us were swimming against the tide, while clinging desperately to the boat. At that point, my main worry was my shoulder bag, which contained my camera, wallet, travellers cheques, passport and address book. We all took turns to dive in search of my precious belongings, but without success. I had visions of having to stand in endless queues, trying to renew all that was missing.

As we were pushing the upside-down boat back to the beach, we thought it might be safer to try to right it to its proper position and with one big heave we successfully completed the manoeuvre. My bag was still in the boat, floating in a few gallons of salty South Pacific sea water! After a two-hour swim

*Hank B Marvin convincing me that Aussie wines are best, 1990.*

back to shore, the boys fell asleep on the beach, totally exhausted, while I hung my documents out to dry!

We were fools to attempt what we did and if we hadn't all been strong swimmers and kept calm throughout, there could have been disastrous consequences. After fifteen trips to Australia, I have taught myself to always be aware of any dangers in the sea. I still have back pains from my body-surfing lesson and I only board a boat to sail with people of experience. Butch has had a yacht for a few years now and has shown me the all-important things to do to make sailing enjoyable and he gave me the following list of things to be aware of, when on board:

1.   Make sure there is enough booze aboard.
2.   Double check there is enough booze aboard.
3.   As soon as the sails are up, serve the drinks!

After spending many happy days watching him become a very good captain, I have become an exellent steward.

When Butch finally decides to hang up his Fender Strat, you will find him tinkering about on his boat in his beloved Cornwall. Where better?


Although we were always coming up with good ideas for singles, we always hit a brick wall when it came to them being broadcast on the radio. *Mr Rubik*, *Blackboard Jumble* and *Du Wot* all had sales potential, but unfortunately they ended up on the wrong pile at Egton House, home of Radio One. However, in the March of '83, we were close to having another big hit. Our last comedy single for CBS had been *Buffalo Bill's Last Scratch*, a spoof on Malcolm Mclaren's *Buffalo Gals*. It was released in February, while we were in Australia, which didn't help matters as it meant that we weren't around to do any promotion for it. We received a call to say that the single had entered the top fifty and to be prepared to go from Gatwick Airport to the TV studios, on our return, to record 'Top of the Pops'. As it wasn't the easiest song to perform live, we spent hours working on a routine that was good enough for the cameras but, after a thirty-six hour flight, we were greeted by Tony who told us that the show was off because the record had stayed at number 49!

Paul Russell, Obie's replacement as chairman at CBS, was annoyed to say the least and demanded an explanation from the promotion team as to why they had let it slip. It wasn't entirely their fault; because we were overseas, the only back-up they'd had from us was a phone-in with Peter Powell. That single was one of our little gems and we were sad that it got lost in the crowd.

We felt that the record company were beginning to lose interest in us after what had happened with 'Buffalo', a great single which did not get the recognition it deserved. With fourteen singles and six albums released, we hadn't done so badly and so we shook hands and parted company. We had had a fantastic run of success from 1977, felt established for life as Britain's top comedy group and we had sold more comedy hits than anyone else. Although I miss the pressure involved in completing an album, we felt no sadness or regret when we ended our partnership with CBS: we couldn't have wished for a better record company.

By the mid-Eighties, there appeared a pattern to our year, which seemed to be a ski holiday in early January, a tour of Australia until April, a theatre tour, another break, summer dates, over to the Middle East, a CSE tour and then the hard slog of 'one niters' and company functions leading up to Christmas.

Our theatre tours became most important to us and were a luxury after battling with the late night cabaret audience; so we planned our shows accordingly, always choosing our support act with care. Usually comics were the best choice as they put the folks in a laughing mood. Andrew O'Connor, big Dave

Lee, Lew Lewis and Duggie Brown were some of the best comics this country has to offer. To get laughs with factory floor humour is easy, but to stand in front of a thousand people and be funny without being blue is a dying art: those names that we chose all had that quality, which is hard to find in these modern times.

We know our place in this fickle business. We're a bunch of nearly middle-aged men, singing Rock'n'Roll and may I say, we're in good company, but it amazes me when I find out who comes to watch us.

Jeff Beck and Led Zeppelin's John Paul Jones watched our act in Tunbridge Wells and they certainly didn't come to watch my guitar playing! All the same, we felt very honoured.

AC/DC lead vocalist, Brian Johnson brought his wife and family to our Newcastle gig and gave us a surprise when he informed us that at every sound check, they sing a Barron Knights song!

'I dont want to go to work, on me bike in the rain.'

With no records in the pipeline, Butch wanted us to change direction. We had a glut of material which he felt could film well for a one hour TV Special.

After a series of meetings, he and Tony squeezed £60,000 out of Channel Four. Cecil Korer, the commissioning editor, had been at 'Top of the Pops' in the Sixties and was quite happy for Butch to produce a good show. We asked Keith Beckett to direct us as he'd worked for Thames TV on a Benny Hill series, so we knew that we were in good hands. Most of the location filming was done around the Leighton Buzzard area, but our live stage show was filmed at the Hexagon, Reading.

For a first attempt, it was a great effort and the proof of our success was in the ratings, when we made number one with the highest viewing figures of Christmas '84! It was repeated at Easter '85 and again it made the top slot. Channel Four were

*Where there's muck there's music. Channel 4 TV.*

173

*With the Godfather, Tony Avern. Northern Ireland.*

happy to pay up again, so we kept the same formula for the show, with repeated success.

It was a tough time for Butch as he helped to write the songs, produce the music, find the locations and costumes, as well as being part of the performance. He lived on his nerves and very little sleep, but always managed to keep his cool when others around him showed their frustration.

After the third show, we realised that we had used over fifty songs from our past albums and felt we needed a rest to take stock, as our source of ready material was drying up. Meanwhile, Jeremy Issacs had taken over at Channel Four and his commissioning editor decided that this new broom was going to sweep clean. So, after three top-rated shows, we were out. It was a blow to us all, but Butch felt it more than us, because of his initial involvement. Again our profile had shot to a high point and it kept the 'bums on seats'.

## Barron and Tony Depart

Three weeks before the Christmas of '84 Barron and Tony called a meeting to inform us that they were leaving the band. It didn't come as a shock to anyone, as there had been conversations which had indicated that they 'wanted out'. Barron had been in a strange frame of mind for a long time. He hated hotel life and lived in a mobile home whenever we stayed away from home. After only ten years of marriage, he and Val had divorced and life, for him, had come to a standstill. He didn't enjoy the TV work and live shows were just a pain for him. He met Roni, his new lady who came from Fiji, through a mutual friend in Sussex, and she had helped Barron through quite a traumatic period of his life. Not knowing what to do or where to go, he was only sure that he wanted a rest from show biz.

Veronica suggested that she did a farewell party for him at our home, so after much thought and deliberation, we decided to have a 'This is your Life' evening. I spent many a frustrated hour on the phone, contacting his old mates, but in the end we managed to get all and every one. His last show was at Stafford on the 27th September, but the party was to be held on the 5th October, the Barron Knights' 25th Anniversary. I rang Barron to ask him to attend a little dinner party for himself, Roni and his dear aged mother and told him it was Veronica's way of saying 'Bon Voyage'.

That night, I looked out into the misty darkness and spotted Barron and Roni pushing Mums up the driveway. As he rang the bell, I whipped the door open, Dave and Butch lifted Mums and the wheelchair into the lounge, while I carried a red book and in my Eamonn Andrews voice said, 'You thought you were coming to dinner, but you were wrong, cos tonight, Barron Anthony, "This Is Your Life".'

I had taken all the paintings off the walls and replaced them with pictures of Barron 'through the years'. He sat in the chair and faced seventy people, mostly old friends and then greeted, one by one, his old buddies from all walks of life. Chris Tarrant, Joe and Vickie Brown, Ted Rogers, songwriter Mitch Murray and many more re-lived some happy memories, while Rolf Harris and Cliff Richard sent recorded messages; at 5 am he was still catching up with his old buddies.

Barron's departure from the band was naturally a sad occasion. He had given up a career in the RAF to form the Barron Knights and his guidance had helped us to become unique. When he reflects back on his twenty-five years, he must feel proud of how it all unfolded: he saw lots of success and very few failures. Where would the rest of us be without him?

Tony, like Barron, left amicably, but had several reasons for wanting to depart.

The pressure on him was that he hated having to come to the office in Leighton Buzzard. For the first few years, the office consisted of just one room; then we bought a house that had been converted into offices. It looked great and was extremly spacious and comfortable, but Tony hated that even more. So we had rented two small rooms for his last ten years. During two periods in his management career, Tony had to get on the phone and sell; one at the beginning and the other at the end. From October 1960 until around mid 1963, he had to launch us into new areas, but then we became a draw and the phone started to ring. In July 1964, when *Call Up The Groups* hit the charts, his main job was to say 'no'.

With all of the hits that we had up to 1971, Tony's main function was to co-ordinate the years' schedules. When the hits dried up, every town had a great nightclub, so live work wasn't too much of a problem. From '77 until '84 we were riding our second crest and once again, selling us was easy; the hard part was trying to please all five of us who were on the road!

The early Eighties saw the closure of many of the nightclubs and the Civic Theatres were feeling the tail end of a recession, so the phone didn't have that nice ring to it any more and Tony thought the business was collapsing. For the first time in a long while, he had to go out and sell and he found it very difficult. Our price was high and he wouldn't budge! Other businesses had lowered their prices, houses dipped in value, cars were cheaper and other artistes had lowered their fees to get the work, which he thought was bad policy. Including the office staff, we had nine mouths to feed, so we had to get the work somehow. Tony thought the end was nigh, so he quit!

He also received a rousing send-off. As he was a mad boxing enthusiast, we had a Fight Night Out at the Grosvenor Hotel in Park Lane. One by one, all the legends of boxing came up to say hello: Frank Bruno, Henry Cooper and John Conteh were the first in line.

On his last day in the office, we were away working, but when Veronica took him a couple of bottles of wine so that the staff could say 'Cheerio', he advised her to pursuade me to retire before things got worse. For me, things were great!

Barron jetted off to New Zealand for a couple of years, where he and Roni ran a wind-surfing school. Each time we worked in Auckland, he would bring a healthy looking crowd with him to see the show.

Tony, for some reason, has never been near any of our shows since he left. I have 'phoned him on the odd occasion, but he's made no attempt to attend any performance. I'm sure he would be proud of what he helped to create and perhaps surprised at the fact that we are still successful. To sever a relationship with five partners after twenty-five years of reasonable success must be a tough task. It will always remain a mystery to me why he did. If he ever decides to come to a show, his old pals would give him a heck of a welcome!

When Tony left, we knew what had to be done. Dave filtered slowly into the management side, before finally swapping his sticks for a mobile phone and with heavy marketing and promotion, we improved our business by fifty per cent. But we decided that we should all get more involved in the management side of the business, in some way or other. As the office was in Leighton Buzzard, we had been aware of the day-to-day running of the band and how the system worked. However, to deligate work, away from the performing side, can be a delicate task as some are good at one thing, but perhaps hopeless at something else.

Butch is our cash flow man, keeping a tight rein on our outgoings and stamping hard on any unnecessary spending and

*Giving Tony a good send-off. Grosvenor House Hotel, 1985.*

*His favourite pastime. Butch at the helm. Sydney harbour, 1988.*

every month he reports on our financial position. He also loves the television projects and having secured the Channel Four deal, he was devastated when they decided not to renew the contract. He definitely worked beyond the call of duty to make those one hour Specials so successful.

Duke is in charge of sponsorship. Hi-tec footwear was his first conquest; trainers, sailing shoes, track suits and T-shirts were all free to us in exchange for an advert in our brochure. His biggest scoop by far was a new motor car! He wriggled his way into the executive suite of Vauxhall Motors in Luton and demanded a top-of-the-range car in which we could travel around. His line of reason was that we were a local band and should be supported by a local company! Mr Alan Mackay, the man in charge at the time, agreed to supply us with a new Carlton every twelve thousand miles, but with our names plastered down both sides of the vehicle, it was like travelling in a goldfish bowl. The saving this made to our business was enormous, and in return we performed a couple of charity shows at Vauxhall and attended the Motor Show.

Although Duke is the one who is crazy about motor cars and motorbikes, who'll stay up all night to watch Nigell Mansell and who took on the job of our 'transport manager', it seems rather unfortunate that he has been relieved of his licence on three occasions by the Bedfordshire Constabulary!

My responsibility is for securing record deals, either for new tracks or the re-packaging of old hits. I also like us to maintain a high standard of performance and sing in tune. Our theatre show is two hours long and I enjoy trying to keep the balance right between comedy and straight singing; but this can really only be achieved by trial and error. However, once I've planned it all, the rest of the boys know that there will be little chance of alteration.

With Dave's move from drum stool to management chair and close consultation between us all, the saying that 'Too

*Duke's had a trike since he was three.*

many cooks spoil the broth' is hardly true in our case. In fact our recipe seems right for long-term success.

# *The Sixth Change*

We had known Bill Coleman for a few years and he'd actually featured on many of our records when he'd played as a session pianist. His main instrument however, was bass, so when Barron left, Bill was the first person we asked.

He was a small, bespectacled chap who rather resembled Arthur Askey. It didn't take him long to learn the show, but he did have problems learning the moves and smiling in the right places, but it all fell into place after a while.

He'd been musical director for Harry Secombe and Helen Shapiro, so joining us was rather a culture shock for him, but his sense of humour was on a similar plane!

At 3 am one morning, half an hour from his home near Market Harborough, Bill swerved to avoid a fox. He and the car ended up in a ditch and he layed motionless for an hour before help arrived. His kneecap was broken and he had to spend a long time recovering in hospital. The press constantly rang his ward to see what progress he was making, but the reporter from the Sun asked the same question, on the hour, 'Is he dead yet?'

Bill made a big effort to become a Barron Knight and he developed good writing skills. A small percentage of our work consists of corporate functions and we are often asked to write something relevant to the company that is signing our cheque.

Whether it be about personnel or product, Bill never failed to come up with a couple of gems.

Our personalised performances for companies became very well known by the agents who specialise in setting up conferences, hence we secured some very interesting dates and venues.

Lada motor company flew us and all the equipment to Barbados for two shows at Sam Lord's Castle. The costs must have been enormous, but a mere drop in the ocean to them. We did the same for Peugeot in Basle and IBM in Brisbane. Singapore Airlines have flown us to Singapore on two occasions; once to launch a new Champagne in First Class and the second time to introduce the Megatop 400 jumbo jet. But our all-time favourite of this area of work was for Rank Travel in 1987.

The ABTA conference was held in Innsbruck, Austria, so we decided to use the *The Sound of Music* as the theme for the show. It took eight weeks to write and rehearse and then, four days before the trip, Bill had his encounter with the fox. We felt so sorry for him after all the work he'd put in to the show.

Apart from pantomime, it was the first and only time we had worn props for our show. We dressed as nuns, walked on stage and sang new words to the songs from *The Sound of Music*. It was our most successful corporate show, but as luck would have it, the recording equipment broke down so we have nothing to show for all the hard work.

One of the strangest requests for a song came from the makers of 'Jeyes', the toilet-cleaning liquid.

We sat in a bedroom at the Excelsior Hotel, Heathrow Airport, and we were stuck in a rut. Then with twenty minutes to go before the start of the show, Bill came up with these words to the tune of *Mame*:

*Innsbruck, 1987. The hills were alive, with Barron Knights.*

185

Who keeps the drains of Great Britain clean? Jeyes
Who keeps your pipes from smelling obscene? Jeyes
Whose famous product helps to shift the nasty things that
 might offend?
In toilets you excel – in fact your way of thinking's really
 round the bend
Who cleans your bathtub, bidet and sink? Jeyes
And helps to kill that old pen and ink? Jeyes
In fact where germs come into it you really make their lives a
 misery
You're always there where they abound
Your Jeyepine sends them all to ground
Who'd be a germ when you're around? Jeyes

It was a superb piece of parody writing and written under pressure.

## *The Seventh Change*

Dave was finding the going tough. Trying to come to terms
with the management of the band, as well as performing, was
taking its toll. It was time to take on another drummer.

All the recordings for the Channel Four programmes were
done at Pace Studios in Milton Keynes, where the owner/
engineer was Nigel Pegrum, long time drummer with Steeleye
Span. While the two of us were attempting a late night mix, he
confided that he would give anything to be in a band like the
Barron Knights. So once again, as with Bill, we didn't have to
audition any other person because we knew that Nigel was not

only a great drummer, but a character well-liked by the rest of the team. He hadn't long been married to his Australian wife, Carmel, and had future plans to live in her home town of Cairns, Northern Queensland. Although we were looking for a long-term commitment, it was as sure as eggs were eggs that one day he would be off. Like Butch, he had Welsh blood in the family and so their make up was very similar: very sensitive towards other people's weaknesses, always nervous before a show, but they always came up with the goods when needed most.

When we cross the border into Wales, we know we're going to return having had a few laughs. They certainly know what hard times are all about, but at the same time, they love to get out to a show and enjoy themselves.

In the autumn of 1974, we had a full house at the Swansea Theatre. It was one of those nights when, if you even moved a finger the audience would laugh. We took our second bow after the encore and the compère came running on stage, grabbed the microphone and stopped them applauding. He then gave a mini speech.

'Ladies and Gentlemen, tonight you have witnessed the greatest act that Britain has ever produced. Why don't you stand up and sing to them the Welsh National Anthem.'

With that, the whole audience stood up and from their big Welsh lungs sang *We'll Keep A Welcome In The Hillside*. I stood on stage with a chill zipping down my spine; it sounded wonderful.

Back in the dressing room, we were in the state of undress, when this middle-aged gentleman burst in.

'I just thought I'd let you know that I brought a coach load of forty people to see you tonight,' he said in a very strong Welsh accent. We all thanked him and then he came out with the classic line, 'Two of them didn't like you!' With that, he shut the door and was never seen again.

At 'Savvas' Club in Usk, we were involved in the usual session of signing our merchandise, when a man in his mid-thirties came to me and said, 'Smashing, you were bloody smashing, you cheered me up.'

'Thank you,' I said, 'you're very kind.'

'Yes, you were smashing, you made me very happy.'

'Thanks mate,' I said, trying not to repeat myself.

'Oh yes, you cheered me up and made me very happy; do you want to know why?' The Welsh accent got stronger.

'Why?' I asked. He came closer to me and in a softer voice said, 'My brother died at half-past six.'

Trying hard not to change any expression on my face, I offered him my condolences.

In 1987 we decided to have another go at summer seasons. We had avoided them for such a long time, but felt it would be a good idea to come off the road for a few weeks and relax by the seaside. We chose Weymouth and for several reasons: it was only an eight week booking, just five nights a week and one show a night. It proved to be a great choice. We broke all attendance records and every member of the band fell in love with the town. The sailing was good for Butch, I enjoyed my golf and Duke found a watering hole to keep his voice in trim!

We had a very talented young comic on the show, who had the sunburned audiences rolling in the aisles. Shane Ritchie was on the first step to stardom.

We worked hard on our PR during those eight weeks; never refusing to open a fete and joining in the local Carnival did the band great favours and played a big part in creating a good relationship between the townsfolk and us. A summer season for the performers, is not just a case of turning up for the show and having a drink afterwards. The locals are the ones to please first then they relay to the holiday makers just which show is the best in town.

We repeated Weymouth in '91, when Bradley Walsh was our support comedian and the show, surprisingly, turned out better than the previous one.

The 'après show' sometimes got out of hand. Our meeting place was the Roundhouse Restaurant, about a hundred yards from the theatre, where the two beautiful hostesses, Barbara and Linda refused to close until the last person had left. It was usually Bradley, who only had to crawl up the stairs to his room on the top floor.

Veronica and I often spend a couple of free days at the 'Roundhouse'. We have a window table and watch the yachts sail into the harbour; we play a couple of rounds of golf at Weymouth Golf Club, where again, we're greeted like long-lost friends. Then we drive back to Bedfordshire, feeling quite sad, as though we're leaving home.

Although we felt, at this time, that our writing was reaching a high standard, having left CBS it was a tough task securing a record deal.

We celebrated the 40th Anniversary of the D–Day landings with *The Churchill Rap*, probably the most intelligent track we have ever recorded. Bob England's Towerbell label offered a deal, but again no response from Radio One.

We had two more attempts at being ultra commercial. *Mr Bronski Meets Mr Evans* and its video version had a few TV airings, but *R-r-rock Me Father Christmas* wasn't broadcast enough; the BBC wouldn't air it until a week before Christmas, far too late for any sales.

We were all convinced that our last three records were our best. Maybe as we were getting older, we were losing touch with what the record-buying public wanted; or could it be that the DJ's feared losing their credibility if they played a comedy

*The new formation with Nigel Pegrum, left, and Bill Coleman, front left.*

record? Roger Pusey, a Radio One producer was once in charge of 'Roundtable', a programme where a panel reviews the new releases. When I asked if he would consider me as a panel guest, his answer was, 'That's more than my life's worth.'

These are the problems that are faced when you become part of the history of British pop music. Producers want young blood and that's both understandable and healthy for the trade we're in. We've done it, twice, but I want to do it a third time! We could have the concert tours for the rest of our lives, but to have a hit record is a very special feeling.

Apathy is something that has never troubled the Barron Knights. We are constantly changing the act as it gives a 'bite' to the performance when a new routine is introduced. Dec Clusky, from the Batchelors, told us that they once called a meeting to discuss the apathy in the group, but nobody turned up! There was never any sense of urgency with the three Irish lads. At the Blackpool Opera House, when they were due to open the show, as the overture began to play over the tannoy in their dressing room, John began to wash his hair!

During the Gulf war we wrote an anti-Saddam song that was a modern day version of *Call Up The Groups*. We went to the studios of the BBC Overseas Department and sang the whole thing live to the troops. No record company would touch it, in fear of a backlash, but we did send a cassette to our DJ friend in Bahrain, the mad-cap Geg Hopkins. On the first day, he played it three times and the radio station was besieged with calls from people asking where they could buy the record. After the programme, he was summoned to the board room, where his Arab bosses were waiting for him. He was in big trouble, but thank goodness he kept his job.

Another of Geg's unfortunate mishaps occurred a few years ago, when as he sat in the studio waiting for the news to finish, he heard the newscaster announce that Bing Crosby had passed away on a golf course in Spain. He rushed to the record library and grabbed a Bing album and just had enough time to place the needle on the first track. He had no idea what the song was called as he said, 'How sad to hear that we have lost a legend. Let's hear from the great man himself.' Over the radio came, 'Heaven, I'm in heaven . . . '

# *The Nineties*

We had ended the 1980s with a tribute dinner from the Variety Club of Great Britain. It was the last thing that we expected and a great surprise to us all. The Brighton Entertainment Centre laid on a great spread while a wonderful speech from our long time, songwriting mate, Mitch Murray had the audience in fits. John Bly from the 'Antiques Road Show' spoke about our value and what we would be worth in a hundred years time and to follow all that was none other than Frank Carson. He spoke for twenty minutes and I'd never heard laughter like it. I laughed so much myself that I must have missed most of his gags. Cliff Richard and the Shadows, Bob Monkhouse and Ted Rogers all passed on tribute videos. It was a great occasion.

The Nineties began with a kick in the teeth! We were cruising along nicely, with a very successful tour of the Middle East and Hong Kong. For convenience sake, we had handed the job of booking our venues to an agent with whom we had worked before and who knew the area. However, our trust in him was entirely misplaced as we discovered that our money had completely disappeared! He'd collected every penny and payed off his other debts, leaving us short of more than a few thousand pounds.

After further investigation, we found that the Bentley he drove wasn't his, the block of offices he boasted about belonged to his accountant and he didn't even own a rabbit hutch. We will never see that money again and although we could have sacked staff and made other cutbacks, we decided to work twice as hard and bite back at the loss little by little. This was the last thing I needed five months before Tanya was due to get married.

With the recession biting hard, we were frequently hearing about acts with little or no work and clubs and theatres that were closing. We sat down and discussed the situation more than once and the answer, as far as we could see, was to get out on the road and see how much we were really worth. A door deal is the only way to find the true fee. If we relied on working only when someone phoned, we would all have to find other work to compensate.

We decided in which parts of the country we had been most successful, then contacted the local theatre or hotel, suggesting the best time of year for a show and the ticket price, then got down to the heavy promotion. Every newspaper within ten miles of the town would get a phone call from one of us personally, that would normally secure a feature and photo. Local radio would then be contacted to organise a phone-in a week before the show; but most important of all, poster sites would be checked. Ninety per cent of our shows have been performed before a capacity audience since this method began.

★

*Dave Lee Travis never fails to help us on our Macintyre Charity Days.*

I believe that it was fate that decided who would be in the Barron Knights. We could never pretend that we do not argue and I admit to being the one who puts his point over the strongest, but it's usually a passionate plea to maintain our high standard. Two minutes before a show we can be engaged in deep discussion, sometimes involving quite hurtful statements, but the moment the curtain rises, we can still light up the stage and give the crowd a happy, fun-filled show.

We have, in the past, seen other bands arrive only twenty minutes before they are due on stage. They walk on, check the microphones with a quick 'one, two, three', leave the stage after an hour and disappear out of the back door. We care about the whole set-up: how close the audience is to us, the lighting and many other details including asking the manager if there is something of local interest that we could write a verse about. This is all part of good marketing and also, by trying to do everything to the best of our abilities, we are kept on our toes and appreciate one another's talents as individuals. I'm sure this attitude has been partly responsible for us staying together for so long.

We are a gang! We do things that gangs do, such as never letting a member forget an occasion that made him look foolish!

While we were at Tito's Club in Majorca, we stayed at a beautiful, family-run hotel called the Monte Crespo. Most of us had our wives and families with us, enjoying the Mediterranean warmth, but Duke had his Mum and Dad in tow! At breakfast one morning, his father said, 'Richard, why don't you spend the day with your mother and I on the beach? I don't understand why you want to laze around the pool all day with those dancing girls and drink all that beer. It's a lovely beach. The sand goes . . . all the way down to the water' (howls of laughter in the breakfast room) 'and you can play on the pedaloes.'

We have quoted those lines to Duke a million times!

Butch performs a very funny sketch with a champagne cork! Holding the cork in his eye, rather like a jeweller does when examining a diamond, his punch line is, 'I think it's some sort of virus.'

One night when the corks were popping, it was rather predictable what would happen next, so Duke grabbed a cork and, out of sight of Butch, he blackened the end that would go in the eye. Butch spent the rest of the night walking around with a black eye! We never did find out what Duke used to blacken the cork, but the next morning Butch couldn't understand what the hotel receptionist and the waitress were laughing at . . . until we gave him a mirror!

I have never been allowed to forget a particular song I wrote entitled *Easily Pleased*. The first lines were;

> She doesn't mind if we live in a wigwam
> By the side of the road
> Have to learn the highway code.

I admit that it is a dreadful piece of work which the lads have sung in many styles: Frank Sinatra, Bryan Ferry, the Stones and many more have been impersonated using my song. One Christmas, they gave me a present of an album called *The World's Worst Record Show*. It was a selection of songs chosen by Kenny Everett and on the front was a sticker saying 'Including *She Doesn't Mind If She Lives In A Wigwam* by Pete Langford'.

Barron, Butch, Duke, Dave and I, with Tony in the management seat, stayed together for twenty five years. It was inevitable that the day would come when the partnership would dissolve. But we were lucky that the three of us that were left were the front line so it wasn't a major problem making the changes.

Bill and Nigel fitted in very quickly and surprisingly very few people noticed anything different. The strain of being away from home took its toll on Bill; and Nigel did eventually go and live in Cairns, so once again we were lucky to find two more good guys. Bass player Garth Watt-Roy and drummer John Shearer have made us musically more close than we've ever been. Garth came from the Q Tips, Paul Young's old band and John previously smashed away with Iron Butterfly and Steve Hackett. Butch and I have had to sharpen up our playing. I've started to use all the fingers on my left hand!

Twenty five years ago, we hired a young skinny lad to be our roadie. He hardly spoke a word then, in fact a dodgy jack plug made more noise! Doug Saunders is still with us but now likes to be called our 'Technical Engineer'. His job is tough. He drives the truck to a gig, sets up the gear, mixes our sound, breaks it all down after the show and drives back home. On show days, he works an eighteen hour day and we've yet to hear him complain. If there was a drinking competition, my money would be on Doug who's known as the Jimmy White of the pub circuit, because he sinks everything from any angle quicker than anyone! I still regret the last time he and I had a jar together. On the 4th October, 1991, we were performing for the Lords Taverners in Hong Kong. After the performance, we were sitting with Greg Chappel and Phil Tufnell when I received a note asking me to ring home. My daughter had presented me with a grand-daughter, baby Eve, who had arrived five days earlier than planned while I was thousands of miles away. I was so thrilled but not so happy about being in Hong Kong at such a time. Butch joined us for a drink that lasted until sunrise! I think I fell into bed for a few hours and somehow managed to get to the Kowloon Cricket Club by midday, where the manager, Ian Powell, had organised a little celebration before we had to rush to the airport and home. I had the head of all heads, but Doug didn't even bother going to bed and was still drinking as we were coming in to land at Heathrow.

On the strength of Doug's talents, we rarely do a sound check in a night club. Arriving an hour before the show, we tune the guitars, check the layout of the stage and on we go. Ninety-nine times out of a hundred the sound will be as good as the venue allows.

On one particular day when a sound check was vital, we arrived to find Doug sitting on the stage with a needle and cotton in his hand. Having found a hole in his trousers, underneath the crotch, he proceeded to sew up the hole while he was wearing them! An hour later, when he went to the toilet, screams of laughter could be heard coming from the tiny room. He had managed to sew his trousers to his underpants, so as he lowered his trousers, his underwear had no choice but to follow. Three hours later, after the show, he came to the dressing room and announced, 'Lads, I thought I'd better tell you that I have to go to the hospital on Monday.' We all looked worried, wondering what was wrong.

'I'm having the stitches out!'

Doug will always be known as the silent Barron Knight.

# The Car Crash

Michael Black, our friendly Jewish agent, had booked Tom O'Connor and us to perform for a toy company in Harrogate on the 23rd March, 1992. We very rarely stay in a hotel after the show, as we prefer to travel home during the night when the roads are clear, rather than wake up to a three hour drive in thick traffic.

The weather was very wet and windy when I took the wheel to head south and I found the car was tough to handle in the wind. As usual, we swapped drivers at the Nottingham service station. Then, as Duke took the wheel, I strapped myself into the front passenger seat and fell asleep. Butch had been asleep since leaving Harrogate.

We both suddenly awoke to the noise of a skid and an awful thud. The silence became a deafening roar, until I heard Duke asking what had happened. I hadn't a clue where we were except that we were upside down and water was all around me; broken glass was caught in my curly hair and it was pitch black. wriggled one hand free and released the strap that was trying to strangle me. I then crawled to the back seats and out of the door Butch had opened. By now, my eyes had adjusted to the darkness and I could see exactly what had happened. We had careered off the road, hit the bank of a ditch, flipped upside down and hit a tree at about sixty miles an hour.

Duke was still groaning in the front seat so Butch and I tried to open his door, but it was stuck. Butch then climbed back into the car and managed to open it from the inside. I pulled Duke out and then both doors slammed trapping Butch! Within a few minutes, we were all standing on the side of the road, shivering and wondering what to do next.

A lorry driver pulled up to let us know that help was on its way, thanks to a milkman on his float who had seen it all. Apparently he drove a mile to the nearest telephone and called the police and ambulance. I then realised where we were; we had just left the M1 at Newport Pagnell; we were only ten minutes from home.

Before we could gather our thoughts, the fire brigade, police and ambulance arrived together. We were soaking wet, covered in mud, there was blood on my face and hands and the

*The wreck, 1992.*

ambulance driver said, 'Bloody hell, it's you lot. I saw you at the California Ballroom, Dunstable in 1960.' He chatted about the old days for about ten minutes before asking us if we were OK and we sat in the ambulance heading for Milton Keynes Hospital, laughing our heads off. We could have needed a blood transfusion or some pain-killing injection, but that seemed to be of secondary interest to our past performances. The driver realised what he'd done and began to laugh with us. It will be hard to forget his big round happy face, a most welcome sight.

The hospital made sure that we were fit enough to go home, where I had a hot bath plus a couple of double gin and tonics. I spent until 6 am picking small pieces of glass from my hands, face and worst of all, my hair.

Next morning, Michael Black rang the office to speak to Dave.

'How are the boys? I've just read about it in the Telegraph.'

'Fine,' Dave said. 'No bones broken just a few little scratches.' The next line could only have been said by a show business agent.

'Thank God it didn't happen on the way to the show.'

I went to survey the car a couple of days later and we were very lucky to come out of it with a few minor cuts and bruises. Without a doubt, safety belts saved our lives.

# *A Proper Job*

Mainly because of media coverage our business has acquired an image of insecurity. It is true to say that certain pop stars and actors have made fortunes and then blown the lot. Those stories sell newspapers and for every success you read about there are a hundred failures. However, the combination of success and good management of financial affairs gives our profession a wide scope for development.

We have always run our affairs on a proper business basis, with targets to reach, promotion and marketing to attend to, always trying to raise the standard of our shows. For years, we've had pension plans, private medical schemes and kept a check on where every penny is spent, as well as knowing who hasn't paid on time. People seem surprised when I tell them that we're a business.

The question we are most often asked these days is, 'How long will you keep doing it?'

Again we're back to the concept of our profession. Would a bank manager be asked the same thing? This is a career for any person who is dedicated, who can take the rough with the smooth, is able to cope with the public's demands and, most important of all, has a long-term attitude. There are so many avenues to explore all of which can pay handsome dividends, providing the correct approach is applied.

From learning to play your instrument, you progress to performing and with the application of your talents you can move on to composing. The natural path from this is the recording studio, record deals and publishing. Record companies, agencies and publishing houses are full of ex-performers. There may be a time when Colleges will offer training for a career in show business. It has a large financial turnover and long may it continue! – That's why we 'keep doing it'.

We travel the world, make people laugh and get paid for it. Offer to pay me double to be a bank manager and I'd say, 'No.' I haven't got the brains.

There is no reason in the world why we should think of retiring. It's too late in life to start thinking about a new career and I've never heard Butch or Duke ever suggest such a thing. Sometimes, when we've had heavy administrative meetings, making decisions on future planning, etc., we leave the boardroom like zombies; but that night we have to do a show. Although it can be a struggle to get wound up, once we're on the stage we forget the world; it's as though we've been injected with a drug to 'lift' us. Butch has often come off stage and, in a 'Doddy' voice, said, 'By Jove, I needed that!'

The show can have the same effect as sailing or golf: your mind is totally absorbed in what you are doing to the exclusion of everything else.

We've always fought shy of television, mainly because producers seem to find it difficult to film a comedy band, but I would like to see the Barron Knights continue performing until well past the year 2000! As the years drift by, we are all singing and playing better and our comedy is certainly claiming bigger laughs than ever before. The great comics like Max Wall, Eric Morecambe and Tommy Cooper took years to develop an act that the public could warm to. It has taken us years to develop routines that are timeless and that work in all four corners of the world and we want the public to appreciate our thirty years of searching and experimenting.

If I could be granted one wish for the band, it would be for a different mode of transport. Travelling the British roads is a nightmare, so it would be wonderful to be 'beamed' to each venue in the manner of 'Startrek' and Dr Spock. How would people like the Crazy Gang have handled the transport system of today, I wonder? In those days, when every town, big or small, had a railway station, it was usual to travel everywhere by train. We battle with juggernauts, caravans and the dreaded double yellow line! Our one advantage over the old days is being able to travel late at night. Whether we're in Manchester, Bristol or Brighton, we always travel home after the show to enjoy the luxury of waking up in our own beds, in our own time and not for the convenience of a noisy chambermaid who wants to clean the room before 8 am.

When I sit and quietly reflect on our achievements, I can't think of anything that we could have done better, except maybe more TV appearances; although there are acts that are continuously on TV but only play to theatres a quarter full! Perhaps being more successful in the States would have been fun, but then again, the demands and extra pressures that might have entailed could have tilted our lifestyle the wrong way. Signing to a big agent may have given us more exposure for a short period, but on the other hand this would have involved giving away more of our earnings, so that move was always questionable.

Some of the records we made and certain sections of our Channel 4 TV shows were lacking in humour, but we fell into the trap of sacrificing quality for quantity. To produce a yearly album full of hilariously funny songs is impossible, while filming eighteen musical comedy sketches of a high standard in three weeks is only fantasy!

Forever the optimist, I have always believed that life can turn a full circle more than once and each year I look forward to better things. I'm not prepared to coast along on the glory of our past achievements and I am more proud than ever of our show at the present moment; it has such resilience that sooner or later we will be 'top of the ratings' once again.

We have worked so hard to make our show the best of its kind in the world. The trend these days is for the easy option of being smutty, at which type of humour audiences will laugh very hard. But there are millions of other people who want a quality family show and I hope we can continue to cater for that market.

Yes, I'm lucky to be working at something I enjoy very much. The grass is always greener . . . you can be mega-rich or poor; you can be so famous that you're always hounded by the press or you can be totally unknown. The Barron Knights fit somewhere in the middle! Enjoy the show!

## *To Conclude*

When you're riding high on adulation, you are at your most sensitive and after a thousand voices have shouted for more, it only takes one adverse comment to bring you down from the clouds and back to the level of normality.

Our 1993 tour of Australia was, without doubt, our most successful. All the shows were sell-outs and the reception we received made us feel rather wonderful, so our walk became a swagger. We drank lots of champagne and we all flew to New Zealand with a healthy looking tan.

After our opening night in Auckland, I was approached by a well-oiled Scotsman.

'What a fantastic night,' he said in his drunken, clipped accent. 'You won't believe this, but I came to see you in a ballroom back in Ayr twenty-five years ago tonight. I know, because I met my wife on that night and you always revive such fond memories every time your records are played on the radio. I can't believe that we saw you tonight; its been a great evening. However, I was very upset you didn't sing your biggest hit.'

'Which one was that?' I enquired. He looked me in the eyes, put his hand on my shoulder and said, 'Lily the Pink.'

So you see, after thirty-three years of sweat and toil, I still call a Coca Cola a Pepsi!

# *Reviews*

No doubt we've had bad press somewhere in this world, but I've yet to come across it. The critics have always been good to us throughout our career. I sometimes unfold the scrap books and read what they've said about us. It reminds me that complacency is fatal. These are a few on which I like to reflect to help keep our standards high.

### Bournemouth Pavilion

It's the jolliest show ever seen at the Pavilion since it opened in 1929. The zest, fun and innocuous mimicry of the Barron Knights have never been better. *The Stage*, 1966

### The Palace Theatre, Brighton

Quick fire comedy spattered from the Barron Knights. Their act was an eye opener in polished professionalism. Rosemary Harris, 1968

## Talk of the Town

One of the funniest all round entertainment acts to play London's
Talk of the Town – That's the Barron Knights, who after their non-
stop 50 minute performance on Monday night must be ranked as a
world class night club attraction.

The pace is hectic and always sustained. There is never a dull
moment from the opening routine to the final song. They have a
superbly clear amplification system and made some listeners think
they were miming but I was assured later they weren't. They are all
good comedians. I hope to see them back many times.

Andy Gray, *New Musical Express*, 1969


## The Three Arts Theatre
## Cape Town, South Africa

The Barron Knights can mix hard rock music with as funny a routine as
I have seen on this stage. The audience warmed to them immediately
and by the end of their act the whole theatre was stomping.

Ted Partridge, *The Times*, 1974


## Bulawayo, Rhodesia

The audience was in fits of laughter and joined in whole heartedly
when prompted. The Barron Knights were as fine a bunch of
entertainers as ever appeared on any stage. They were slick, comical,
and they knew their music. In fact they are members of a dying breed
known as entertainers.

Their whole act had that easy formality, the result of painstaking
rehearsals, which deservedly had us all shouting for more.

*The Sunday News*

## Weymouth Pavilion

The Barron Knights have attracted record crowds for their six week summer run. Attendances have been double what they were last year.
The Barron Knights have more than proved that after all these years they still boast a large and loyal following. They bring a touch of television into the theatre by making their show sparkling.
Andrew Wyllie, *Dorset Echo*, 1987


## New Zealand

The Quintet had the crowd in raptures with their self-effacement-take-no-prisoners humour. While to a large section of the audience they were preaching to the converted, the spontaneity and enjoyment they put into performing marks them as a special act.
Everyone in the audience was affected or overcome by their music. Nigel Benson, 1990

# The Barron Knights
# Complete Discography

## SINGLES

| | |
|---|---|
| Fontana H 368 | Let's Face It/Never Miss Chris |

| | |
|---|---|
| Columbia DB 7108 | Jo-anne/That's My Girl |
| Columbia DB 7188 | Coming Home Baby/Peanut Butter |
| Columbia DB 7317 | Call Up The Groups (Parts One and Two) |
| Columbia DB 7375 | Come To The Dance/Choose Me Tonight |
| Columbia DB 7427 | The House Of Johann Strauss/She's The One |
| Columbia DB 7525 | Pop Go The Workers (Parts One and Two) |
| Columbia DB 7698 | It Was A Very Good Year/Worry And Wonder |
| Columbia DB 7780 | Merry Gentle Pops (Parts One and Two) |
| Columbia 7884 | |

Round The World Rhythm And Blues/Where There's A Will There's A Way

| | |
|---|---|
| Columbia DB 7933 | Doing What She's Not Supposed To/Every Night |
| Columbia DB 8071 | Under New Management (Parts One and Two) |
| Columbia DB 8161 | Lazy Fat People/In The Night |
| Columbia DB 8280 | Here Come The Bees/It's A Sin |
| Columbia DB 8423 | I Will Never Marry/A Cold In My Nose |
| Columbia DB 8485 | An Olympic Record (Tracks One and Two) |
| Columbia DB 8612 | |

Love And The World Loves With You/Along Came Those Summer Days

| | |
|---|---|
| Columbia DB 8679 | Traces/Awake |

| | |
|---|---|
| Plexium PXM 21 | If You Jumbo Jet Me/Peaceful Life |

(This was a protest track under the name 'Wings Of A Dove'. We were against a third London Airport being built at Cublington, three miles from our home town.)

| | |
|---|---|
| Penny Farthing PEN 768 | Hey Ho! Europe/I'm Gonna Give My Love To You |
| Penny Farthing PEN 777 | Popumentary 72 (Parts One and Two) |
| Penny Farthing PEN 786 | You're All I Need/Nothing Doing |
| Penny Farthing PEN 797 | To The Woods/Turning My Back On You |
| Penny Farthing PEN 818 | Turning My Back On You/Oh Little Girl |
| Penny Farthing PEN 854 | The Ballad Of Frank Spencer/Pardon Me |
| Penny Farthing PEN 881 | Danny's Song/Me And My Guitar |

(This was a solo recording under the name of Pete Langford).

| | |
|---|---|
| Tavern STA 1007 | |

Hatters Hatter/We Are Luton Town You Know (With The Luton Town Squad).

| | |
|---|---|
| Epic SEPC 5752 | Live In Trouble (Parts One and Two) |
| Epic SEPC 5981 | Back In Trouble Again/Autograph Hunter |

| | |
|---|---|
| Epic SEPC 7603 | Get Down Shep/Give Me Something To Ease The Pain |
| Epic SEPC 6829 | A Taste Of Aggro/Remember – Decimalisation |
| Epic SEPC 7048 | Boozie Nights/The Big V-Asectomy |
| Epic SEPC 7791 | The Topical Song/Evolution |
| Epic SEPC 8011 | Food For Thought/Nanu Nanu |
| Epic SEPC 8780 | We Know Who Did It/Herbie The Head |
| Epic SEPC 8994 | The Sit Song/Barrons Fun Forty |
| Epic SEPC 9070 | Never Mind The Presents/Swindon Cowboy |
| Epic EPC A 1596 | Mr Rubic/Fads And Crazes |
| Epic EPC A 1795 | Blackboard Jumble/Gobbledegook |
| Epic EPC A 2872 | Duwot?/Spaghetti Betty |
| Epic EPC A 3208 | Buffalo Bill's Last Scratch/Centrefold |
| Epic EPC A 3892 | Full Circle/The Eye Of The Hurricane |
| | |
| Towerbell TOW 54 | The Churchill Rap/The Loan Arranger |
| Towerbell 12TOW 54 | The Churchill Rap/The Loan Arranger (12″) |
| | |
| Scratch SP 123 | Mr Bronski Meets Mr Evans |
| | |
| WEA VZ 92 | R-r-rock Me Father Christmas |
| | |
| Big Wave BWR 26 | What A Mix Up |

## EP's

| | |
|---|---|
| Columbia SEG 8424 | Guying The Top Pops |
| Columbia SEG 8526 | Those Versatile Barron Knights |
| | |
| EMI 2697 | Call Up The Groups + 3 |

## LP's

| | |
|---|---|
| Columbia 33SX 1648 | Call Up The Groups |
| Columbia SX 6007 | The Barron Knights |
| Columbia SX/SCX 6176 | Scribed |
| | |
| Penny Farthing PGC 1012 | One Man's Meat |
| Penny Farthing PAGS 533 | Knights Of Laughter |
| Penny Farthing PELS 536 | One Man's Meat |
| | |
| Tavern MTA 1001 | Songs From Their Shows |
| Tavern STA 1003 | Barron Knights |
| Tavern STA 1005 | Odds On Favourites |
| Tavern STA 1010 | The Barron Knights |
| Tavern STA 1015 | The Barron Knights |
| Tavern STA 1016 | The Barron Knights |
| Tavern STA 1017 | The Barron Knights |
| Tavern STA 1018 | Limited Edition; The Barron Knights |
| Tavern STA 1019 | Easy Listening |

| | |
|---|---|
| Epic EPC 82451 | Live In Trouble |
| Epic EPC 83221 | Night Gallery |
| Epic EPC 83891 | Teach The World To Laugh |
| Epic EPC 84550 | Jesta Giggle |
| Epic EPC 85319 | Twisting The Knights Away |
| Epic EPC 25707 | Funny In The Head |
| | |
| Pickwick SHM 981 | Knights Of Laughter |
| Pickwick SSD 8037 | The Two Sides Of The Barron Knights |
| | |
| Contour CN 2052 | The Barron Knights |
| | |
| Warwick WW 5128/9 | The Best Of The Barron Knights (Double Album) |
| | |
| Spor SPR8510 | Live In Trouble |
| | |
| Wea 600 135 | California Girls |
| | |
| BKS 1001/CBKS1001 | Don't Let The Germans Pinch Your Sunbeds |

## CASSETTES ONLY

| | |
|---|---|
| The Anniversary Album TTMC 074 | The Best of Barron Knights (Double) |
| C5 C5K572 | The Two Sides Of The Sensational Barron Knights |
| Pickwick | The Best of Barron Knights |

## COMPACT DISCS

| | |
|---|---|
| SRT92CD3437 | Latest And Greatest |
| C5 CD 572 | The Two Sides Of The Sensational Barron Knights |
| Pickwick | The Best Of Barron Knights |

## VIDEO

| | |
|---|---|
| AK Music 001 | Get Knighted |

This Discography is complete up to July 1993.

The cassette and CD on the C5 label are the Penny Farthing tracks and the Pickwick 'Best Of' cassette and CD is exclusive CBS material, including all the hits from the Seventies and Eighties.